25 in 10

Twenty-Five Ten-Minute Plays

Compiled and Edited

by

KENT R. BROWN

Dramatic Publishing

Woodstock, Illinois • England • Australia • New Zealand

For Linda Habjan and Char Borman who have graciously
provided invaluable insight and expertise.

25 in 10

TABLE OF CONTENTS

LITTLE SINS

By
Susan Cinoman

Little Sins was part of an evening of one acts entitled "Instabilities," produced at the Theatre Artists Workshop of Westport, Conn., in 1997.

CHARACTERS

SHERI: An attractive suburban woman.
JOHN: An attractive suburban lawyer.

SETTING: John's well-coordinated law office.
TIME: The present.

LITTLE SINS

AT THE CURTAIN: *SHERI has just entered JOHN's office.*

SHERI. Hi.

JOHN. Come on in.

SHERI. Nice desk.

JOHN. Thanks.

SHERI. Is this the one that Julie picked out for you? Now where was that? Crate and Barrel... Oh...hold everything... oh I know... wasn't that House of Desks?

JOHN. Yeah.

SHERI. Right. Right. House of Desks. So.

JOHN. So.

SHERI. So, I brought my party planner. So shall we plan the party? the big 4-0, marching toward oblivion and all that? Did you make your list?

(JOHN clears all the papers off his desk with a firm sweep of his arm.)

SHERI. Oh. Uh-oh. What did I say? You're angry, right? You were in court this morning. I know how that can be for you. Because Julie tells me. I know that must be super stressful. So, I guess you're feeling a little worn-out, maybe a little violent. Umm...we can talk about the surprise party another time.

JOHN. I don't want to talk about the surprise party.

SHERI. Oh.

JOHN. I want to make love to you.

SHERI. Oh. You mean ... on your desk.

JOHN. Right.

SHERI. Which is now clear. Free and clear. Of papers. Because that's why ... I mean, hence you're sweeping-off-of-the-papers action.

JOHN. Ha.

SHERI. Oh. You're kidding, right? Because we've all been such good friends for so long. And you and Mark play racquetball. And I mean he's my husband and Julie is your wife and she's having the party so this is your way of saying surprise to me, too. Like a joke. Like a big joke. Right?

JOHN. I knew what you wanted last year when you gave me the cigar humidor.

SHERI. Uh-huh.

JOHN. That was a very expensive gift.

SHERI. You're telling me.

JOHN. And Mark never knew. Did he?

SHERI. Well you know about Mark and money. I call him Roger Chillingsworth on that subject. You know that. He and his money are as close as, well ... close.

JOHN. I know that I make you nervous.

SHERI. Right now you do. Yes.

JOHN. I want you very much.

SHERI. Wow.

JOHN. Very much.

SHERI. Huh.

JOHN. Does that surprise you?

SHERI. Well it wouldn't have. In college. But three children later? I mean, "I want you" is usually followed by ... "to make me French toast" or " ... to get off the phone..." but "I want you on the desk," that's sort of like a distant cry from the past...like a little voice of a siren on an island far away. I'm not saying it's bad.

JOHN. You have no idea who you are, Sheri.

SHERI. Umm...that could be. But I know who you are. A very successful tax attorney who is friends with everyone in this town, a veritable athlete, a member of not one but two country clubs... I couldn't even get Mark to blow up an inflatable pool in the backyard last summer. Why would you risk everything for a fling with me?

JOHN. I'm not talking about a fling. I really want you. I haven't thought about anyone but you for a year.

SHERI. Come on.

JOHN. I'm not interested in a seduction. That's just my style. I don't know how else to communicate to you that I have this need. This need...

SHERI. For me?

JOHN. Sheri, look at my office. Look at me. What do you see? Perfection?

SHERI. Gee, John...

JOHN. Everything in order, control. Look at the way Julie and I have done our house, our calendar, our lives. Order, precision, everything right and beautiful and pristine. And then look at you.

SHERI. Oh.

JOHN. I mean...that's what's so wonderful. You're so out of control. You were supposed to be here an hour ago.

SHERI. I was? I didn't know.

JOHN. How could you know? You don't wear a watch! Do you know what that does to me. I lie awake at night thinking Sheri Brown doesn't wear a watch. How is she going to get her kids to soccer practice tomorrow. How is she going to time her chicken? Can she even tell time? These things don't matter to her. What is she thinking about? Maybe she's thinking about the ocean, its limitlessness, and about death and the elusiveness of our reality. Maybe the reason that she can't put on a new sweater without wearing the store tags around for three days is because her mind is on her own voluminous passions. Her passions have swept away all of her reason and all of her practical sense. And I think how can I enter that disorderly unconscious world of hers and become free? I must enter her, that's how. And that's why I'm willing to risk everything to be with you. Because all of that craziness that you are, Sheri, is worth it.

SHERI. Wow.

JOHN. Don't make me beg.

SHERI. What an interesting twist of fate. I remember when I used to wait by the phone hoping that it would ring.

JOHN. You waited for me to call you.

SHERI. I waited for Julie to call me. She was always so cool and blonde. "If she were my friend," I'd think, "I could get through the day." And now here is her cool husband desperately wanting me on his lunch break. Huh.

JOHN. That's what I mean. Only you could answer my advances with such an odd response. Come here.

SHERI. I...

JOHN (*pulling her toward him and kissing her*). Please... don't be frightened...

SHERI. Mm... you look so nice in that suit. Is it a Ralph Lauren?

JOHN. Don't be defensive. You're wild. Everything about you has wildness in it. I even see it in your little Jenny.

SHERI. My... what do you mean?

JOHN. I see your wildness in Jenny. I see it in her when she comes to play with Katherine. I look at Katherine, she controls all of their play. It's Katherine's game and Jenny, little animal that she is, gets pulled forward by her leash.

SHERI. Are you talking about my daughter, Jenny, or Buck, the sled hound?

JOHN. Ha! Kiss me again!

SHERI. Umm...wait a second, John. I'm a little distracted. Are you saying that Jenny doesn't behave when she comes to your house?

JOHN. Shhh...

SHERI. Because I've never heard any complaints about Jenny's alleged wildness. Sure she's got an active imagination but...on the other hand, your Katherine is disliked by a lot of kids for her bossiness. Kids don't like to be bullied, you know.

JOHN. Your child is beautiful.

SHERI. Well OK.

JOHN. Naturally Katherine is the achiever.

SHERI. Oh? I wouldn't confuse aggression with achievement, John.

JOHN. Well no. Neither would I confuse imagination with an inability to focus.

SHERI. Oh really?

JOHN. We're just being parents. Let's not be for a moment.

SHERI. Well...no. Let's just finish this discussion. I'm sort of not at all in the mood anymore.

JOHN. All I'm saying, sweetheart, is that lack of discipline in a child and doing well in school really don't go hand in hand.

SHERI. Yeah. Well neither do we...

JOHN. Sheri...you're being impetuous.

SHERI. I thought that was what you were after.

JOHN. Yes. But a moment's consistency wouldn't hurt.

SHERI. OK. *(She sits on the desk.)* Well?

JOHN. I...I'm thinking.

SHERI. Wouldn't you just. So...are we going to do it?

JOHN. Yes. Of course we are.

SHERI. Then you'll admit that your little slur of Jenny comes out of a basic jealousy that you have for my child compared to your child?

JOHN. I don't think so.

SHERI. Oh I do.

JOHN. I want you, Sheri, but you're mistaken. And Jenny is your third. Surely after your first two disasters you and Mark might have learned from your mistakes.

SHERI. Mark is a good father! Maybe if you spent a little more time with your daughter like he does...you wouldn't have to find fulfillment through the seduction of other people's wives!

JOHN. Like you.

SHERI. All I wanted to do was plan a party for your poor wife.

JOHN. I think I know what my wife wants a bit more than you could.

SHERI. Not from what she tells me.

JOHN. Oh? If you thought that I was missing something in that area then why were you so willing only moments ago?

SHERI. I don't know. I wanted to be surprised. And besides even though you have a rotten kid...I like your desk.

(SHERI picks up her party planner and exits.)

END OF PLAY

THE BLOCKING MANEUVER

By

Seth Kramer

The Blocking Maneuver premiered at the Word of Mouth Theatre's "15 Minutes of Fame" Festival, New York City, 2000. The play was directed by Taylor Ruckel and featured Kevin Rehac and Kim Winter. The piece was included in the Turnip One-Act Festival produced by the American Globe Theatre, New York City, 2001. It featured Chance Muehleck and Larissa Kiel, and was directed by Melanie S. Armer.

CHARACTERS

DRILLING: Age 30-50. Scruffy, tweed jacket, professor-type. False modesty.

GRETCH: Younger than Drilling. An eager, obsessive, "starstruck" fan. Hyper—edging toward manic.

SETTING: A bar.

TIME: Anytime other than morning.

THE BLOCKING MANEUVER

AT THE CURTAIN: *DRILLING and GRETCH sit at opposite ends of a bar. They both have notepads open. GRETCH agonizes over her pad, hating every word. DRILLING writes, possessed. GRETCH looks at DRILLING a few times. DRILLING pops a piece of nicotine gum. His pen dies. Pause. DRILLING shakes his pen a few times.*

GRETCH. Pen?

DRILLING. Hmm?

GRETCH. Do you need— Your pen seems to be out of—

DRILLING. Oh, right. *(Takes pen.)* Thanks.

GRETCH. My pleasure.

DRILLING *(beat)*. Umm.

> *(GRETCH stares at him. They exchange a nod, and smile. DRILLING goes back to writing.)*

GRETCH *(leaning in)*. You're him. *(Beat.)* Aren't you?

DRILLING. Him?

GRETCH. You're... no, I know who you are.

DRILLING. I...

GRETCH. No, you're—you write that—come on—I recognize you from the picture on the dust jacket— I can't believe this—I am such a big fan of yours. A really BIG fan. I can't believe I'm even sitting next to you. Wow, this is—this is a real honor. I've read everything you've ever written. Everything. *(Conspiratorially.)*

Even that sci-fi Erotica novel you wrote under that pen
name. I got a copy off eBay. I think you're *great!*

DRILLING. Um... thanks.

GRETCH. I can't believe this. This is so cool. I'm Gretch.

DRILLING *(shakes her hand)*. Gretch, OK. My name is...

GRETCH. Hey, come on!

DRILLING. Sorry.

GRETCH. Didn't we just have a conversation?

DRILLING. Reflex... sorry. Nice to meet you, Gretch.
(They shake hands again.)

GRETCH. An honor. Really. *(Beat, sly.)* The guuuuuum.

DRILLING. Pardon?

GRETCH. Used to smoke three packs a day, right? Camel
Unfilters.

DRILLING. That's right.

GRETCH. Now you're doing the nicotine gum. I read
about that online.

DRILLING. It's all these fascist no-smoking laws. Is this
America or isn't it? Can't smoke in restaurants, can't
smoke in bars or hotel lobbies. Hell, one day they're
gonna be telling actors they can't smoke onstage. Then
where will we be? Move to Europe, that's where.

GRETCH. That's so... insightful. Wow.

DRILLING *(sizing her up. Beat)*. You... You want a
piece?

GRETCH. Me?

DRILLING. Sure.

GRETCH. Ah, come on!

DRILLING. It's OK if you do.

GRETCH. For true?

DRILLING. Absolutely.

GRETCH. Don't mind if I do. Thanks. That's quite "Common Man" of you. *(Beat.)* Should I just...just take a piece myself then?

DRILLING. Go ahead.

GRETCH *(pops a piece of gum)*. Thanks. Well. Well, then. OK.

(They chew together. DRILLING leans in.)

DRILLING. "All the Nicotine—Twice the oral satisfaction."

(The two laugh a little.)

GRETCH *(beat, confides)*. You know, I quit last year, too.

DRILLING. You did?

GRETCH *(rolls up sleeve, shows patch)*. The week after you. Patch and everything. A real bitch! I gotta wear two of these damn things just to feel normal again, know what I mean?

DRILLING. Oh.

GRETCH. This gum's really got some *pep*.

DRILLING. Maybe you shouldn't do both...

GRETCH. Are you kidding? Like I'm going to say "NO" to you. Get real.

DRILLING. I think it's kinda dangerous to...

GRETCH. For all I know you get half your ideas from the nicotine rush, right? Maybe I just patch and chew my way into the next great American novel. Hell, maybe it's sitting down at this end of the bar. The right end of the bar. "*write* end" of the bar. Get it?

DRILLING. Uh-huh.

GRETCH. Little wordplay there.

DRILLING. I got it.

GRETCH. Just a couple of writers, some blank pages, pens and ideas. Can't beat that, can you? *(Pause, DRILLING tries to write again.)* So...so...sooooo...do you mind if I ask...

DRILLING. What?

GRETCH. What'cha working on there? Another bestseller?

DRILLING. I don't like to talk about it.

GRETCH. No?

DRILLING. No.

GRETCH. 'Fraid I'm gonna steal your idea, huh?

DRILLING. Oh, no, nothing like that. No. No, I didn't mean to...

GRETCH. It's OK.

DRILLING. I just don't want to jinx it.

GRETCH. Sure.

DRILLING. That's all.

GRETCH. I understand.

DRILLING. Superstitious, you know.

GRETCH. It's going well, then?

DRILLING. Uhhh...

GRETCH. I'm not trying to pry.

DRILLING. Not at all.

GRETCH. Just, you know, one writer to another.

DRILLING *(bragging a little)*. It's gone worse.

GRETCH. Ahhh—this guy! "It's gone worse"—Nobel Prize worse, I bet.

DRILLING *(enjoying this)*. Well.

GRETCH. No that's great. I'm—really—yeah, good.

DRILLING *(beat)*. And you?

GRETCH. I'm not sure.

DRILLING. No?

GRETCH. I'm not—that is to say—*unhappy* with how things are going. I've had it go better before, that's for sure. A *lot* better before...

DRILLING. But you're getting it on the page.

GRETCH. I guess.

DRILLING. That's what it's about, right? I mean, if you're not writing then you might as well not be breathing.

GRETCH. Well, that's a bit militant.

DRILLING. You think?

GRETCH. For me, yes. For *me*. But then, hey, who the hell am I? You're the one who's rolling right along. You're "Getting It Down." You're "Doing the Work." Who am I to say...

DRILLING. Look, I didn't mean to...

GRETCH. No, I'm the one who...

DRILLING. I apologize if—

GRETCH. ...who is rambling on at you. At *you*—I mean—you've been on the bestseller list— Interviewed in *Entertainment Weekly*. (*Beat, with awe.*) You've been *Oprah*-fied. (*Beat.*) ...*and* right now you are on a *roll*. Jesus. I should just shut this hole under my nose and go away. Leave the *artist* to his *work*. I should take my "hobby," my "tinkering," and stop distracting you.

DRILLING. Well...

GRETCH. I should, shouldn't I? (*Beat.*) It was nice meeting you. An honor. Thanks for the nic-fix. I'm gonna go.

DRILLING. No.

GRETCH. No?

DRILLING. I'm not trying to...I don't mean to seem...

GRETCH. What?

DRILLING *(forced)*. I can...talk to you about it, I guess.

GRETCH. You can?

DRILLING. For a little while, sure. *(Puts cap on pen.)* A break. It won't kill me.

GRETCH. That's very...

DRILLING. But only for a *little* while. OK? When I start to...

GRETCH. No, I understand. I totally—thank you. Thank you for taking this time.

DRILLING. Sure.

GRETCH. So.

DRILLING. So.

GRETCH. So, can I see it?

(DRILLING hands GRETCH the pad. She reads.)

DRILLING. Now it's only a first draft. A *handwritten* first draft. You understand what I'm saying? I never usually...

GRETCH. A love story?

DRILLING. Uh-huh. I never do this.

GRETCH. You're writing...

DRILLING. Yes, a love story. *(Beat.)* I never let a fan see my writing at this stage. So lucky you, huh? Kind of exciting...

GRETCH *(reads with growing distaste)*. Umm.

DRILLING. Just like you. See? Little marks on the paper. The story gets written one word at a time, see?

GRETCH. This is sorta a departure for you.

DRILLING. It's what's inside me right now.

GRETCH. I guess that's the important thing.

DRILLING. You know, I have a few other chapters back at my home office. If you're interested, we could...

GRETCH *(beat)*. Hetero?

DRILLING. Well, yes. Although I am open to experimentation if...

GRETCH. Your story.

DRILLING. Ah. I thought you were asking...this being a bar and all.

GRETCH. Oh please, I'm a *fan* not a *groupie*.

DRILLING. I didn't mean to say...

GRETCH. Get a little bit of fame and...

DRILLING. The story is. Yes. The story follows a man and woman through their...

GRETCH. Commercial then. *(Beat.)* What am I saying? Of course it's commercial. You're *you!* The public consumes everything you put on paper. A boy meets girl in the park—something or other—swelling music moment—typical love story. Wow.

DRILLING. Typical?

GRETCH. Did I say that?

DRILLING. Yes.

GRETCH. I meant to say hetero.

DRILLING. You said typical.

GRETCH. Well Freud me up the ass and slip my tongue! Excuse me. I should have one of my fingers broken for even suggesting—placed on—*typical*—the rack. That was inexcusable.

DRILLING. I mean, no story is *typical*.

GRETCH. You even wrote that in one of your "writer pontificates about writing" books, didn't you?

DRILLING. Don't you think?

GRETCH. I meant to say hetero. *(Beat.)* Although...

DRILLING. What?

GRETCH. No. Nothing.

DRILLING. What?

GRETCH. I should just—just shut up and let you get back into it. Back up on your wave. Here. *(She hands the notepad back.)*

DRILLING. Well...all right.

GRETCH. You'll figure something out.

DRILLING. I know the whole plot already.

GRETCH. Oh, you work *that* way.

(They both write for a beat. DRILLING stops.)

DRILLING. I'm curious...

GRETCH. Yeah?

DRILLING. What were you going to say?

GRETCH. It's just... *(Gestures to gum.)* May I?

DRILLING *(gives her pack)*. Sure, here.

GRETCH. I've seen it before.

DRILLING. You have?

GRETCH. Yeah, the hetero thing. It's a bit—been there—done that. That's all.

DRILLING. Huh.

GRETCH. It's cliché.

DRILLING. Well, I—huh... *(Beat.)* Cliché?

GRETCH. Danielle Steele.

DRILLING. I hadn't...huh.

GRETCH. But, you know, "No story is typical," and all that crap. Right? *(Beat.)* So you just get back into it and I'm sure it'll sell when the time comes. After all, you are you. *(She starts writing in her own pad.)*

DRILLING. Yes. I... *(Beat.)* You really think it's typical? *(GRETCH nods.)* Really? *(GRETCH nods.)* They don't meet in a park, you know. They meet in a graveyard. It's a very dark story. I think...that's different, right? A graveyard. A love from beyond the grave. *(GRETCH shrugs.)* Well, maybe...this isn't set. Nothing is in stone. I could, bring in a...another person. A mailman or football player or circus clown. It could become a triangle-type thing. With a murder. A circus clown, sex, murder, that's...

GRETCH. Seen it.

DRILLING. But—but...the idea was...if I... This is only a first draft so... There is no such thing as a typical story. It's all about execution. The— *(Beat.)* There is *no such thing as a typical story. (Beat.)* Right? *(He starts and stops a few times.)* So, what are you working on?

GRETCH. Sorry. I'd rather not talk about it.

DRILLING. But I just...

GRETCH. Sorry.

DRILLING. I'm...I'm...hey, you've read everything I've written, remember? I'm world-renowned. Maybe I could help you.

GRETCH. I want this to be original. No offense.

DRILLING. I see.

(DRILLING tries to get a peek over GRETCH's shoulder. GRETCH maneuvers to block his view.)

GRETCH. Do you mind? Person space. Jeez.

DRILLING. Is it a love story? Is that it? A *gay* love story or something? Because I've seen that before too. That's not original either. *(Beat.)* Can't you just tell me a little ...

GRETCH. No.

DRILLING. Well. All right. Well. *(Beat.)* Nice chatting with you.

GRETCH. Um-hmm. An honor.

DRILLING. Good luck. *(Beat.)* I said good luck. *(Beat.)* Well.

(DRILLING stares at his page. He can't write. GRETCH scribbles furiously. Beat. DRILLING opens his pack of gum and finds it empty. GRETCH blows a bubble and never stops writing. Blackout.)

END OF PLAY

CONTACT

By
Doug Grissom

Contact had a staged reading by Mill Mountain Theatre, Roanoke, Va., 1993, and was produced by Offstage Theatre in Charlottesville, Va., 1993, and by Chicago's Studio Theatre, 1997.

It was previously published by *Rockford Review*, Vol. XII, 1993-94.

CHARACTERS

MAN
VOICE

SETTING: A spacecraft of a future century. A realistic set is not required, but there could be some sort of console with which the central character can interact (pushing buttons, flipping switches, etc.). However, even those actions can be mimed, so that all that is really necessary is a chair.

TIME: The future.

CONTACT

AT THE CURTAIN: *A man is seated at the spaceship console. He is talking into a microphone.*

HE. The green beans today were amazing. Leaving them partially frozen gave a simulation of texture which was pretty remarkable. Life-like? Well, ridiculous to think in those terms. After eighteen months or so ... memory doesn't ... the tricks of mind that one plays after ... so long without communication with ... human beings ... are pretty ...
(Pause.)
Did I tell you, oh gentle listener, of my recent romantic episode? It started one day when I was feeling very nostalgic. I started remembering—with startling clarity ... a romance I had when I was seventeen or so. A brief but fireworks-filled encounter. The memory excited me enough that I had an erection. Speaking of lost facilities. The memory excited me enough that I masturbated. Speaking of lost talents. And then suddenly I realized that encounter from my youth ... never happened at all. It came from a dream I had early on in this journey.
(Pause.)
I've developed a bad habit of rambling, haven't I? Or maybe it isn't a bad habit. Maybe it's exactly what you want. Whoever you are. Whenever it is that you find these. If you find ... And anyway, gentle listener, be you from the 21st, 24th, or 48th centuries, I've begun to look forward so much to our little weekly talks.

Well! I suppose you're waiting for my official update crap which forms the centerpiece of these lovely little chats. Fine, so here it is: Been adrift now for eighteen months, one week, three days. Food supply...based on present consuming rates...well, it's now down to...

(Punches up number on console computer.)

...oh my God...I didn't realize it was that low...I only have enough food to last me 537 years. Of course if I keep coming up with more gourmet ideas like leaving green beans half-frozen I may gobble through my food in a mere four centuries or so. And of course the reason for this bounty, in case you missed the other fifty or sixty recordings, is that I am all alone on this vessel equipped for seventy-five people.

(Pause.)

I can't read anymore—did I mention that? Reading was my great solace for the first fifteen months or so. I'm only about one-twentieth of the way through the recreational files. But I can't...reading about people...people who are...with other people...in the world...Earth...when Earth doesn't exist anymore and when the few people left from there are so...scattered and mainly scattered...from me, well...that former life seems too amazingly gorgeous and impossible now. The unreality of that life to me now is so...huge.

(A faint BEEP comes from the console. During the following, he slowly manipulates various buttons, levers, etc., on the console.)

Ah, gentle listener...you're in luck. You get to hear me do something. My scanning device just beeped. Now what that could mean is that there is a spaceship or an inhabited planet in the neighborhood sending out a radio signal... maybe even responding to my radio signal. Now why am I not all aquiver with excitement? Well, because this stuff happens every few days or so and I have learned from long and painful experience that the beep can be triggered by any number of things...meteor showers, exploding stars, intergalactic turds, oh, you name it. But of course I do go through the motions...increasing frequency of my signal, aiming my ears more precisely in the direction of the source, etc.

(Pause.)

There...hear? Nothing. Off the scope. When I first heard the beeps I—was excited of course. Yes, "beeps." Another manifestation of my lack of skill at...I wonder how many lay people are flying these things around the universe... The engineers made them damn easy. Fly. Not a very accurate word, I suppose. Sounds more active than... drift...float.

(Pause.)

The loneliness is...stupid to think about, even. And I'm sure you're tired of me dwelling on...

(Pause.)

Amazing that Earth could have been destroyed in that way. Amazing it could be ravaged and obliterated in such a...silly way. Not what anybody expected. Nobody suspected the fragility of it. Oh, maybe somebody did. I didn't. The masses of people didn't. The masses of people. Imagine that. Details of the obliteration are in Sector I of this disk, of course, if you're interested. I can't imagine why you would be.

(Pause.)

Why do these recordings always turn to that stupid event, or to my own stupid... I should tell you of my wonderful adventures. How I spend my day. How I persist in thinking in terms of hours, days, weeks—how I keep clocks and calendars. How I'm careful to plan my day so that I have enough to do, and don't get finished too soon. The routine maintenance of the ship, my daily jog on the track, my scintillating meals, my weekly date with you, gentle listener. My weekly collapse into any of a wide variety of psychological afflictions...sometimes blind fear, sometimes intense claustrophobia, sometimes horrifying rage, sometimes exquisite self-pity, sometimes simple bland depression.

(Pause.)

Interesting: no matter what my specific affliction is at these times...I always end up the same way physically. I'm crawling, scraping the floor...clawing my skin, my hair.

(BEEP. He glances over, makes a slight adjustment.)

Okay...a new development in the last week. As a way of holding on I started memorizing various technical manuals. I astounded and scared myself at how much I could retain and how little I could understand.

(Pause.)

See? I am trying to hold on...and let go at the same time. I just...need to find some path...

(BEEP.)

That's odd. It's never gotten stronger before.

(BEEP.)

What the hell is that?

(He breathes hard for a second.)

Oh fuck, don't even...

(Pause; no sound. Angrily:)

It's amazing how incredibly...the human organism, of the 21st-century variety anyway, is amazing...just fucking amazing. At the slightest sliver of possibility...hope erupts all over the place...hope gushes out of every sentimental pore of our being. Even though we know the statistical improbabilities...even though we know from hundreds...thousands...of past experiences that there is nothing there—nothing important anyway...still...

(He starts laughing.)

...still some residual soft spot gets all aquiver...gets all fucking weepy with...anticipation...

(Pause.)

...and as long as that fucking happens...only when I start to accept my situation...only then will there be any possibility of...

(Pause. Then a BEEP.)

Quit fucking with me! You're just a fucking meteor!— you're just a fucking intergalactic turd!

(BEEP.)

Will you goddamn quit that!

(BEEP.)

You're nothing!—you're—

(Louder BEEP. He becomes very still. An even louder BEEP. He begins breathing heavily. A louder BEEP. Quietly:)

Please stop this...

(Loud BEEP.)

Oh my God...

(Loud BEEP. He begins flipping switches and punching buttons, but in a careful, methodical manner.)

Okay...now I will just...follow the manual...just in case... just to follow procedure...to just determine for myself...in the interests of science and space exploration, of course...

(BEEP changes tone. It sounds five more times in regular intervals.)

Oh my God...

(Three more in the new TONE.)
... it's from Earth ...
(Another TONE.)
They've got my signal. They're honing in to me.
(Other types of BEEPS and TONES come in a rush.)
A communique. A code ... where's the goddamn translator switch.

(He searches his panel, finds the switch. The TONES switch to a digital voice. [Note: this could be done with a "real" voice from offstage].)

VOICE. ... request information ... request response ...
HE. Yes ... hello—hello!
VOICE. Communique is not clear ...
HE. —hit the goddamn reverse translator, you asshole! *(He hits another switch.)* Hello! Hello!
VOICE. We have contact.
HE. Oh my God— Hello! —Who are you?
VOICE. This is Remrac Ship 872.
HE. A Remrac ... a floating city ...
VOICE. What ship are you?
HE. You're a floating fucking city!
VOICE. Request information about your vehicle.
HE. This is a Tarak—Tarak 7.
VOICE. How many inhabitants.
HE. Me. One.
VOICE. One? In a Tarak?
HE. It's a long story. How many are on your ship?
VOICE. Present occupancy is ... 2145.
HE. Oh my God ... my God ...
VOICE. Is your ship fully functional?

HE. Uh...yes...as far as I know. I'm not really a technician, I...

VOICE. Set your coordinates for vector 9.71. Do you know how to do that?

HE. —yes, I believe so—I mean, that's fairly elementary, right? How far away are you? I can't tell with my...

VOICE. We can rendezvous in approximately five months.

HE. Oh my God...I'm saved...

VOICE. You need to set coordinates and fire booster immediately. Do you understand what's happening?

HE. What do you mean?

VOICE. You have entered into the gravitational field of vector 3977—you are at the edge of our bubble for just an hour or so. If you do not set coordinates and fire booster by that time you will be in a separate gravitational field and will be unable to rendezvous and unable to maintain contact.

HE. Don't worry—setting them right now... I can't believe—can't believe—

VOICE. Suspending communication. Reestablish when you are firing booster.

HE. No—not yet—wait! Who are you?—what country are you from?

VOICE. You need to set coordinates.

HE. I know—but tell me—what's it like there—what do you do—

VOICE. We will communicate on a daily basis until you arrive.

HE. Keep talking now—it's been so long.

VOICE. We have other duties.

HE. Just tell me—what country are you from?

VOICE. Many countries.

HE. What does that mean?

VOICE. Suspending communication, Tarak 7. Resume when coordinates are set.

HE. What country?

VOICE. Many countries. Too numerous to name.

HE. How did you all get on one ship?

VOICE. We are suspending communication. We have vital duties to take care of. All your questions will be answered. Set your coordinates.

HE. No!

(TONE changes indicating suspension of communication.)
Why won't they talk to me? Why won't they tell me anything?

(Pause.)
Why won't they...talk to me? If they're in a Remrac—with that many people—how can they all be too busy to talk to me?

(Pause. Then smiling:)
Oh, of course...they aren't starved for contact...they have all the contact they want!

(Pause.)
Maybe more than they want. Maybe they're crawling all over each other. And what if they don't have 2115 people but...have 3000...or 4000—a Remrac can hold that many. I'm in a Tarak...alone...and can last for 580 years or so. And they know that.

(Pause.)
They could use my food and air. Maybe the last thing they want is another body to take care of. They don't even know what my skills are—they didn't even ask me—could they afford to just take on any new person...out of the goodness of their hearts? In their position another body

would be the last thing I'd want. Food and air would be the first thing I'd want. Food and air which could be gone within ... a few years ... a year. A month. *Stop this—stop it!*

(He tries to gain control of himself. Pause. He savors the words:)

2115. 2115 people.

(Pause.)

A month is enough.

(Pause.)

You hear me, gentle listener!? 2115 people! I'm saved! I'm saaaaaved!!

(He stops abruptly.)

What if they aren't even ... from Earth? What if they aren't even human? What can I possibly know about them from talking to them. What can I possibly know besides ... myself?

(Pause. Loud TONE as before.)

VOICE. Tarak 7. The situation is more critical than we thought. You are farther on the edge of the bubble than previously calculated. You need to fire your booster within the next five minutes. Are your coordinates set?

HE. Yes ... well ... almost. *(He flips switches more rapidly than before.)* Tell me something about yourself.

VOICE. You must do this immediately. Once booster is fired you will be firmly within our bubble. Then we will be able to link with you.

HE. Yes. Whether I want to or not.

VOICE. Repeat, Tarak 7?

HE. I request more information.

VOICE. Information?

HE. Life aboard your ship. Who is there? Where do you come from? Your status on supplies.

VOICE. Supplies are adequate. There is nothing to worry about.

HE. How many years.

VOICE. One hundred and fifty years.

HE. Even with taking on extra passengers?

VOICE. Tarak 7—you must finish setting coordinates and fire booster immediately. Repeat: immediately. *(He flips two more switches.)*

HE. Coordinates set.

VOICE. Firing booster?

HE. You must tell me...

VOICE. What?

HE. Who you are!

VOICE. Tarak 7—you're going over the edge of the bubble. You need to fire immediately!

HE. ...I

VOICE. We lost that, Tarak 7.

HE. Tell me...

VOICE. Fire your booster, Tarak 7! *(He places his hand on the lever.)* Have you fired? Tarak 7!

HE. I...I...

VOICE. Tarak 7!

HE. I can't!

VOICE. Why?!

HE. You're not human!

VOICE. What?!

HE. How do I know—you're human?!

(STATIC increases.)

VOICE. Tarak 7 we are losing you!

HE. Prove to me—

VOICE. Tarak 7!

HE. —prove you're human!

VOICE. Tarak 7—please—you have to—

(The voice disintegrates into STATIC. The STATIC abruptly changes to silence. His hand is still frozen on the lever. He stares into space. Pause.)

HE *(quietly)*. Prove to me...you're one...of my kind... *(Pause.)* Hello?...hello?...

END OF PLAY

MOVABLE PEOPLE

By
Nikki Harmon

Movable People received a staged reading by Milwaukee's Playwrights' Studio Theatre in 1994.

CHARACTERS

MRS. GROSSMAN: Upper 60s to upper 70s.

MR. LANSKY: Upper 60s to upper 70s.

SETTING: A New York City deli, Formica tables, nothing fancy, just good food at good prices. The tables sit by the front window next to the door. One is occupied, the other clean, and set up. Other empty tables may or may not be seen; if they are, there needs to be dirty dishes on them.

TIME: The present.

* * * *

GLOSSARY

ALAV HA-SHOLOM: Literally: On him peace. Said automatically when referring to someone who died.

BAR MITZVAH: The ceremony when a Jewish boy comes of age.

BISSEL: A small amount.

BRIS: The ceremony to circumcise a baby. Family and friends are in attendance and a celebration follows.

ELIJAH: The prophet who it's believed will precede and herald the coming of the Messiah. At Passover a special cup is filled with wine for Elijah and the door is opened on the chance he comes.

MAZEL TOV!: Congratulations!

MESHUGGENEH: Crazy.

TWO-CENTS PLAIN: A splash of seltzer is sometimes added to drinks. This was just a glass of seltzer, plain, that sold for two cents.

MOVABLE PEOPLE

AT THE CURTAIN: *MRS. GROSSMAN is sitting with a bowl of borscht, meticulously wiping her spoon with a handkerchief that she folds and puts back into her purse.*

MR. LANSKY enters clutching an old worn briefcase as if it held the Hope diamond. Looking around, he chooses the table next to MRS. GROSSMAN who's going at the borscht full steam.

MR. LANSKY. I'm going to sit here.

MRS. GROSSMAN. So sit.

MR. LANSKY. I would sit at another table, but the others, the boy hasn't cleaned yet.

MRS. GROSSMAN. I don't care where you sit. You want to sit there. Sit there.

MR. LANSKY. The reason I told you where I'm going to sit is I don't want you should spritz me with the borscht.

MRS. GROSSMAN. Do I look like a person who'd spritz a person with borscht?

MR. LANSKY. I don't want to take a chance.

MRS. GROSSMAN. You're going to a wedding or a *bris* maybe, and you don't want your suit should get a spot? Because if you are, if you don't mind my saying, the suit you're wearing is not what my husband, *alav hasholom*, would have worn to such a thing,

MR. LANSKY. I'm not going to a wedding or a *bris*. I just like to take precautions.

MRS. GROSSMAN. Well, Mister I-can't-get-a-*bissel*-borscht-on-my-suit, I don't spritz when I eat. You can ask anyone. "Does Sophie Grossman spritz when she eats?" and they'll tell you "Never!" Never, in fifty years of coming here, to this place, has a person said "Don't sit next to Sophie, she spritzes."

MR. LANSKY *(looking around)*. There's no one here to ask.

MRS. GROSSMAN. Already, you don't trust me.

MR. LANSKY. I don't even know you.

MRS. GROSSMAN *(pulling a business card out of her purse)*. Here.

MR. LANSKY *(reading)*. Sophie Grossman. *(Turning the card over and back again.)* There's no phone number. No address.

MRS. GROSSMAN. You're a stranger. Why would I give a stranger my phone number and address?

MR. LANSKY. It's a business card. What kind of business card doesn't have a phone number and address?

MRS. GROSSMAN. A card for a person who doesn't do business. What kind of business do you do?

MR. LANSKY. I'm retired.

MRS. GROSSMAN. From what?

MR. LANSKY. From business.

MRS. GROSSMAN. Ho, ho, Mister Smarty Pants. *(She slurps a spoonful of borscht with great determination and spritzes.)*

MR. LANSKY. You spritzed! You said you don't spritz.

MRS. GROSSMAN. So sue me.

(MRS. GROSSMAN continues to slurp her borscht with great abandonment as MR. LANSKY builds a barrier between the two of them with napkins draped over the salt and pepper shakers, the napkin holder and the mustard and relish containers, all the while mumbling to himself.)

MR. LANSKY *(to himself)*. Delis on the East Side, delis on the West Side and I have to sit in one with a spritzer. A hot dog I could have gotten on the corner with people bumping right and left, and there wouldn't be one spritzer. But I come into a deli with one other person and what do I get? A *meshuggeneh* spritzer!

(The "Great Wall of China" is complete.)

MR. LANSKY *(to MRS. GROSSMAN)*. Now, you wanna spritz? Be my guest.

(MRS. GROSSMAN "Humphs" and continues eating, but not spritzing. Content he's won the war, MR. LANSKY opens his briefcase and extracts a bundle wrapped in cloth and tied with string and undoes it. Inside the bundle are old, tattered photos. Carefully, he lays them in rows. Two on top, then three under those, and so on until they're arranged in a particular order, all the while talking to the photos, as MRS. GROSSMAN looks and listens without looking and listening.)

MR. LANSKY *(cont'd)*. An anniversary last week. A birthday soon. Two birthdays past. *Mazel tov!* on yours, and yours and your *bar mitzvah*. A birth. Three weddings, and a graduation. A celebration for all the days of joy. *(Calling out.)* IF THERE HAPPENS TO BE A PERSON ACTUALLY WORKS HERE I WOULD LIKE TWO GLASSES WINE, ONE RED, ONE WHITE AND A TWO-CENTS PLAIN.

MRS. GROSSMAN. Excuse me, but a person drinks without food, this is not good. Now, since I know from the food here I know what is good. The corn beef is good, the pastrami is not and the brisket's the best you can get. So, you have the brisket, a couple thick slices of onion and a pickle and that makes for you a meal. Two glasses wine and a seltzer is not a meal. Trust me. I know.

MR. LANSKY. What can a person eats borscht like a peasant know?

MRS. GROSSMAN. Who are you calling a peasant?

MR. LANSKY. I'm calling a person who spritzes borscht a peasant. *(Pointing to MRS. GROSSMAN's table.)* Look! There! A spot! And there, another! From spritzes these spots come. Not from a spill, not from a dribble, from a spritz they come. And from where I come from a spritzer's a peasant, and from a peasant you don't take advice, because if they knew from what they were talking they wouldn't be a peasant!

MRS. GROSSMAN. This place you come from, this place with spritzing peasants, it has people who play cards with pictures?

MR. LANSKY. I'm not playing cards.

MRS. GROSSMAN. Then what are you doing with them?

MR. LANSKY *(adding napkins to the barrier)*. Right now, I'm protecting them from another barrage of borscht.

MRS. GROSSMAN. I won't spritz again. *(MR. LANSKY eyes her cautiously.)* I promise. *(MR. LANSKY removes one napkin.)* Such a trusting person. *(MR. LANSKY removes one more, but that's it. MRS. GROSSMAN cranes her neck to see.)* The woman in the top picture, the one with the flowers, she's got a pretty face, that woman.

MR. LANSKY. Yes.

MRS. GROSSMAN. And the man in the picture next to her, he's a nice-looking man. Strong features. Good eyes.

MR. LANSKY. Yes.

MRS. GROSSMAN. Before you wouldn't stop talking, now nothing.

MR. LANSKY *(calling out)*. WHAT DOES IT TAKE TO GET A LITTLE SERVICE?! HELLO! HELLO BACK THERE! *(There's no response. MR. LANSKY gets up and swings the door wide open.)* LOOK, EVERYONE! IT'S ELIJAH! QUICK BRING WINE! ONE RED, ONE WHITE AND A TWO-CENTS PLAIN!

MRS. GROSSMAN. I have a seltzer I haven't touched. You drink, and when yours comes, I'll drink.

MR. LANSKY. The seltzer's not for me.

MRS. GROSSMAN. There's someone else sitting here?

MR. LANSKY. It's for my mother, *alav ha-sholom*.

MRS. GROSSMAN. You're ordering a seltzer for your dead mother?

MR. LANSKY. She didn't like wine.

MRS. GROSSMAN. The two glasses wine *they're* for you?

MR. LANSKY. The red is for my sister, *alav ha-sholom*. My wife, *alav ha-sholom*, liked white.

MRS. GROSSMAN. Is anyone alive drinking?

MR. LANSKY. Your borscht is getting warm.

MRS. GROSSMAN. The pictures, I noticed you put them in an order. I like a man with order. It shows a good mind. (*Examining the pictures closer.*) It's a nice looking family you have.

MR. LANSKY. Had.

MRS. GROSSMAN. The picture of the woman, there, by the one with the man in the big hat. Who was she?

MR. LANSKY. My second cousin's wife.

(*MRS. GROSSMAN reaches for the photo but MR. LANSKY stops her, then sees the numbers on her arm and lets her take it. We can see she recognizes the picture, but he's too occupied with the other photos to realize it.*)

MRS. GROSSMAN (*looking closely at the picture*). Her hair is so long.

MR. LANSKY. And red, like a tomato. (*More to himself than to MRS. GROSSMAN.*) No one in the whole town had such hair, and always me and my cousin Meshe and his cousin Sophie would give it a pinch to see if it would rub off. My second cousin would shake his fist at us, but his wife would laugh and grab her hair and rub as hard as she could and say, "See, it doesn't come off," and we'd gasp at such a wonderful thing...and then the war, and I hid like a mouse in a cellar, and people, gifts from God, fed me and kept me, and when it was over the town was gone, all of them, except me... I miss Meshe. I miss Sophie. I miss my second cousin yelling, and if I could see them just once more...

MRS. GROSSMAN (*putting the photo back on the table*). I knew a woman with such hair.

MR. LANSKY. Like a tomato?

MRS. GROSSMAN. A ripe one.

MR. LANSKY. From where did you know this woman? From here?

MRS. GROSSMAN. No.

MR. LANSKY. From where, then?

MRS. GROSSMAN. From before.

MR. LANSKY. From where before?.

MRS. GROSSMAN. From a town.

MR. LANSKY. From what town?

MRS. GROSSMAN (*calling out*). WHAT DOES IT TAKE TO GET A LITTLE SERVICE HERE?! A MAN WANTS WINE AND A TWO-CENTS PLAIN!

MR. LANSKY. A man wants to know from where you know a woman with hair the color of ripe tomatoes!

MRS. GROSSMAN. Sometimes we lose a thing, and when we get it back we don't always like what it is we get.

MR. LANSKY. What are you talking about?

MRS. GROSSMAN. There's an empty spot next to your second cousin's wife's picture.

MR. LANSKY. My cousin Sophie's mother goes there. Now you tell me how you know a woman with such hair.

MRS. GROSSMAN. You haven't a picture?

MR. LANSKY. No, I haven't a picture. The woman, you must tell me...

MRS. GROSSMAN. And under?

MR. LANSKY. Under goes Sophie. But the pictures are gone, like the people. The woman with the red hair, please. You must tell me.

MRS. GROSSMAN. I have pictures, too.

MR. LANSKY. I'm not interested in your pictures. I just want to know ...

MRS. GROSSMAN *(taking a locket from around her neck and opening it)*. Maybe in this one. It's a picture of my mother. *(Placing the locket next to the one of the woman with the red hair.)* It's the one goes there, by her sister ... and I'm the one goes under.

MR. LANSKY. You're Sophie?!

MRS. GROSSMAN *(offering her hand)*. Sophie Rosenbaum Grossman.

(Stunned, bewildered and amazed, MR. LANSKY takes her hand.)

MR. LANSKY *(shaking hands)*. Harris Lansky.

MRS. GROSSMAN. Pleased to meet you.

(Still holding her hand, MR. LANSKY begins to weep as he kisses it gently, and the lights fade out.)

END OF PLAY

DON'T THINK SO HARD

By
Hope Gatto

For Terrence Sherman, who taught me to find the outfield wall ... and then surpass it.

Don't Think So Hard premiered at the Kelsey Theatre, West Windsor, N.J., 1997. It featured Yecenia Torres and Darren Johnson, and was directed by Terrence Sherman. It was subsequently produced by Love Creek Productions in New York City in 1997. It featured Martha Castro and Barret O'Brian and was directed by Merry Jayne Howard.

CHARACTERS

CELESTE: Early 20s and newly married to Alan.
ALAN: Late 20s.

SETTING: The living room of Celeste and Alan's apartment.

TIME: The present.

DON'T THINK SO HARD

AT THE CURTAIN: *ALAN is sitting on the floor of the living room going over bills. Papers are spread out all around him. CELESTE is sitting next to him, reading a book about relationships. They sit in silence for a moment. CELESTE puts the book down and stares at her husband.*

CELESTE. Do you think I'm pretty?

ALAN. You know I do.

CELESTE. I'm serious. Do you *really* think I'm pretty?

ALAN. Of course. Stop acting like a nut.

CELESTE. But do you think I'm beautiful?

ALAN. Yes, you're beautiful.

CELESTE. There *is* a difference between pretty and beautiful, you know.

ALAN. You are pretty *and* beautiful ... simultaneously.

CELESTE. If you had to choose one, which one would you say I am?

ALAN. Jesus, Celeste. What's with you tonight? I think you're gorgeous. There, I said it. It wasn't on the list, but that is the adjective I would choose to describe you. Is that okay?

CELESTE. You're just saying that to shut me up.

ALAN *(under his breath)*. Like that would ever happen.

CELESTE. What?

ALAN. I'm sorry. I'm kind of slow tonight. What is it that you want me to say?

CELESTE. I don't want you to say anything you don't really mean. I want you to say what you think. Honestly.

ALAN. You want to know what I think? I think that you have been spending too much time reading those books that say I'm from Mars and you're from Venus, and the dog is from Pittsburgh, where what I say isn't really what I mean and I have some crazy ulterior motive when I communicate with you. The truth is...I'm too tired to think that hard, Celeste. *(Beat.)* I think you're the most attractive woman I've ever met.

CELESTE. Why didn't you say that I was the most attractive woman you've ever *seen*? There's a difference, you know?

ALAN. Because if I said you're the most attractive woman I'd ever seen, you'd start rattling off names of supermodels and accuse me of lying just to make you happy.

CELESTE. I thought you said you didn't think that hard.

ALAN *(laughing)*. That isn't thinking. That's instinct. Husband survival instinct.

CELESTE. Oh, you're a riot, Alan. You think this is funny? You think not being happy anymore is humorous?

ALAN. Who said they weren't happy anymore? I never said that.

CELESTE. You didn't have to say it.

ALAN. What? Are those damn books telling you that you can read my mind? No wonder those relationship doctors are making millions. They dupe women into over-analyzing every single conversation to death, and then tell you how to create misguided theories behind what men say. There aren't any. Believe me. I'm happy!

CELESTE. Look at us. You call this "happy"?

ALAN. No, I would call this freakin' crazy. That's what I would call it.

CELESTE. It's hard for me to believe that we've only been married five months...not fifty years. Last week, I went out to lunch, and at the table next to me was this old married couple. It was 11:30 in the morning and they were eating dinner. Dinner, Alan. At 11:30 in the morning. They didn't look at each other during their entire meal. They just ate their dinner at 11:30 in the morning in silence.

ALAN. So?

CELESTE. *So*...the guy ordered a big bowl of lime Jell-O, and I watched him devour it with more passion than he had for his wife.

ALAN. Yeah? Well, what was *she* doing while he was committing this unforgivable sin?

CELESTE. I was watching him mostly, but she just sat there and drank her coffee. It was black, and I'm sure it was very, *very* bitter.

ALAN. Well, we don't eat dinner at 11:30 in the morning. I hate lime Jell-O. And we talk during our meals.

CELESTE. Ordering from the menu doesn't count, Alan.

ALAN. We aren't that couple, Celeste. We are us.

CELESTE. You're right. We *are* us, but we aren't the same "us" that existed when we were dating. We don't *do* the same things. We sure as hell don't *say* the same things. We're different people now, Alan, and it scares me.

ALAN. Are you saying that we were at our best when we were dating?

CELESTE. I'm saying that we shouldn't have peaked at all yet. Our finest moments should be in front of us. I want our life together to be an incredible journey toward absolute completion. I want to discover fabulous things about our relationship every day so that every night we can look at each other and say, "Hey, that was great. And guess what... it only gets better!"

ALAN. Maybe that old couple... maybe that *was* their best. Have you thought of that? Maybe for them *that* was perfection. They worked hard at their relationship all their lives so they didn't have to when they got old. They waited fifty years so they *could* have their dinner at 11:30 in the morning... with each other... in *silence*. *(He goes back to his papers.)*

CELESTE. What about the lime Jell-O?

ALAN. Huh?

CELESTE. What about how he slammed down that gigantic dish of Jell-O with more desire than he showed for his wife? And she sat there drinking her bitter coffee.

ALAN. You don't know it was bitter.

CELESTE. Let's *pretend* it was bitter. How do you explain that?

ALAN. Listen, Celeste, if it was bitter she should have put *sugar* in it.

CELESTE. What if she was just all out of *sugar*? What if she had been out of *sugar* for a long time?

ALAN. I think we are getting *too* carried away with the symbolism here.

CELESTE. What if she tried to make little discoveries about her marriage every day to make everything sweeter, but it became too difficult and meaningless to do it alone? That's what I'm talking about, Alan. We get up in the morning. We go to work We have dinner. We watch TV. We go to bed. On Friday and Saturday nights we do "it." You can't unearth fresh and exciting details about one another when your life runs like clockwork. It's like an old, familiar dance. True, we never *stop* dancing, but we don't add any new leaps and twirls either.

ALAN *(slightly offended, he looks up from the bills)*. We don't just do it on Friday and Saturday nights. We did it last night and last night was Wednesday. If you count last week in the shower, that was a...a Friday. Never mind. *(Goes back to his papers.)*

CELESTE. Don't you see, Alan? I don't want to have to count.

ALAN *(pause)*. Is it really that bad?

CELESTE. I'm just afraid, Alan.

ALAN. Afraid of what?

CELESTE. I don't want to talk about it.

ALAN *(forgets bills altogether)*. What?! C'mon, Celeste. What are you saying? I mean really. What are you really saying? Talk to me, Celeste. If you aren't happy, tell me how I can make you happy. Tell me and I will do it. Tell me how to fix it.

CELESTE. If you don't know by now then I'm not going to tell you.

ALAN. You know, I need to get one of those relationship books you read and sadistically memorize because I seem to be totally clueless about this new telepathic way of arguing!

CELESTE. We need to be more aware of each other. We need to get that special look back in our eyes. Remember when we went camping in Colorado. We were lying in that crappy little tent, and it started pouring and we looked at each other and laughed. And *kept* on laughing, looking into each other's eyes, and all of a sudden we started crying. That look we had was so intense and filled with so much love that it literally made us weep.

ALAN. I remember.

CELESTE. We haven't looked for a long time, Alan.

ALAN. Just because we haven't done that lately doesn't mean the feelings are gone. *(Pause. Tenderly.)* You know, the other night when we fell asleep on the couch? I woke up, turned and just watched you sleep. You were riveting. You were stunning and you were riveting. Your eyes were shut so tight that you looked like a little girl about to make a wish on her birthday candles. I put my face really close to yours, and I could smell your peach shampoo and face cream. I loved it. I *really* loved it. *(Pause.)* I haven't looked into your eyes and studied them lately, but I do look at you, Celeste. I do. I'm sorry.

CELESTE. My God, Alan. That was … absolutely … perfect. I've never heard you talk like that about me.

ALAN. I don't always talk like that, but I do *think* like that. I should probably tell you more often what I'm thinking. I … I just never thought about it.

CELESTE. Don't think so hard, Alan. I love you.

ALAN. I love you, Celeste. Always. *(ALAN pulls CELESTE gently to him. They kiss.)*

CELESTE. Alan, we're going to have a baby.

ALAN *(long pause).* I'm sorry. I'm a little slow tonight. What was it you just said?

CELESTE. I'm pregnant. I found out today. It was eight weeks ago … *on a Saturday night.*

(ALAN stares at CELESTE for a moment with no expression. He suddenly lets out a loud, happy yell. He lifts her into his arms and swings her around the living room. He begins to dance with her, twirling and spinning her around.)

ALAN. Oh, Celeste! We *are* going to discover fabulous things together. It *will* only get better, Celeste. We'll choreograph new dances *(Dips her.)* and we'll talk with our mouths full and I'll curse lime Jell-O and...and you'll drink sweet coffee every day of your life. Although caffeine probably isn't that great for the baby. But we'll uncover beautiful things about each other every morning and we'll take all the time in the world at night to explore some more. The baby will give us so many precious moments with each other that we won't even have to concentrate on making quality time for our marriage. It'll just *be* there.

CELESTE *(sarcastically)*. Sure, Alan. It's a known fact that couples actually have *more* time for each other when a baby comes along.

ALAN. I know! Isn't it great?

CELESTE. Well, at least you're going to try. That's all I ask. That you at least *think* about it. *(They embrace and kiss.)* Alan? Can I ask you something? Do you think I look fat? Seriously. Do you think I'm fat...or do you think I'm just a little chunky, because there *is* a difference, you know.

(Blackout.)

END OF PLAY

SACRED GROUND

By

Elaine Berman

Sacred Ground was featured in "Octoberfest," an evening of plays produced by Ensemble Studio Theatre, New York City, 1996, and was premiered by the Theatre of Yale Drama Alumni at the Yale Club, New York City, 1999.

CHARACTERS

LEE GARDNER: Any age from mid-30s on.
ACE BLACKBURN: A little older than Lee.

Both men have charm and the sheen of business people who are accustomed to success.

SETTING: A bare stage with office furniture that includes a laptop desk, desk chair and a round table with two chairs. There are file folders on the table and a laptop computer and a phone on the desk.

TIME: The present.

SACRED GROUND

AT THE CURTAIN: *LEE GARDNER has just entered ACE BLACKBURN's office. Both men are wearing business shirts and ties. ACE's jacket hangs over the back of his desk chair. LEE walks to ACE's desk and stands over him as ACE, hardly looking up, types intensely on the computer's keyboard.*

LEE. You think I'm a piece of shit, right? You do—right? That's what you think.

ACE. I never said that.

LEE. This morning, I didn't want to come in here. I got a knot in my stomach. Not a normal knot. Not a normal, going-to-work-in-the-morning knot. A bad knot. Bad.

ACE. Take something.

LEE. It isn't a medical problem.

ACE. It could be.

LEE. It's not.

ACE. You don't know that.

LEE. It's not.

ACE. When I was a kid, and we saw something messy, we'd say: it looks like vomit, but it's snot. That still makes me laugh.

LEE. It would.

ACE. Oh?

LEE. That's you: body functions—your sense of humor.

ACE. This analysis has to be in at the end of the day—all the numbers plugged in; I'm a little bit behind. *(ACE gets up to get a file folder from the table, turning his back to LEE.)*

LEE. So what does that mean? I don't want to talk about it? Go away? Get lost? Look, I worked up my courage. I came in here. I'm serious.

ACE *(opening a folder).* And you have an analysis on your desk to finish.

LEE. We've been friends for a long time.

ACE. Good friends.

LEE. It's important to me.

ACE. To me as well.

LEE. Years. It isn't a little thing.

ACE. I have this analysis to complete. *(ACE walks to his desk with the folder and sits with eyes only for the papers in the folder.)*

LEE. Have you ever heard the word forgiveness?

ACE. I've heard the word.

LEE. The day could come when you didn't think I was a piece of shit. I mean, things don't stay the same. A person gets mad at a person and then forgives, because a relationship is valued. Sometimes, the relationship is actually improved, because there is a new understanding.

ACE *(looks up).* You're not a piece of shit. You're a pile of shit.

LEE. It wasn't that bad!

ACE. I'm trying to write an analysis, which must be in on time, as yours must be, and I'm not prepared to be totally distracted right this minute.

LEE. I'm trying to write my analysis, and I can't think straight. You didn't say good morning in the parking lot.

ACE. I said good morning.

LEE. A grunt. Not a drop of warmth.

ACE. I'm not happy when I see you.

LEE. It wasn't that bad, Ace.

ACE. It was terrible. Now go away and let me work.

LEE. And I'm a piece of shit, right? Now and forever. I'm a permanent, petrified piece of shit.

ACE. No—petrified things are like rocks. They don't stink.

LEE. There was minimal damage.

ACE. There's a note in my file, damn it.

LEE. I don't know anything about that. I just know you've heard something.

ACE *(becoming involved, turns to LEE)*. You told some stories.

LEE. I was talking about both of us.

ACE. Did they offer you counseling?

LEE. Counseling?

ACE. They offered it to me.

LEE. What?

ACE. Some help. Some support. For God's sake. Yesterday. They called yesterday and offered help.

LEE. Oh no!

ACE. And I said I drink a little wine and a little beer, and I don't need a counselor. My God, what the hell did you tell them?

LEE. The trip to New Orleans. Dinner. We were telling stories.

ACE. And you talked about me.

LEE. Just kidding around.

ACE. Something about how I'm always drunk on the road.

LEE. Have we had good times together?

ACE. Two glasses of wine don't make me always drunk on the road, you asshole. And to a senior vice president?

LEE. No, I...

ACE. Debra quoted you. This is your friend? she said. Some friend. And then the call came from Human Resources.

LEE. Road stories—you know—times we had fun.

ACE. So you give a senior vice president the impression I'm a drunk because it's amusing?

LEE. It wasn't smart. Okay? It wasn't the brightest thing I've ever done. I know that, but I didn't mean to hurt you.

ACE. Careless people can do more damage than the out-and-out louses.

LEE. It wasn't bad enough to be beyond forgiveness.

ACE. Keep your voice down.

LEE. The door's closed. And, Ace, it was about our friendship, about how much fun we have together; I was having such a good time talking about it. This group had been together for a week—all day and into the night. I felt tired and mellow and close to everyone. And he's a nice guy; I forgot he was a senior vice president. I mean, he was just a guy at a restaurant table telling road stories, so I told a few, and they added up to something I didn't mean.

ACE. Am I a boozer, Lee?

LEE. No, of course you're not. Ace, listen...

ACE. What do you want from me?

LEE. Forgive me. Please forgive me. You're the best friend I've ever had in my life. I'd be lost without you.

ACE. You're the best friend I've ever had.

LEE (*going in front of ACE as ACE looks in files and jots notes on a pad*). Talk to me. Friends ought to be able to work their way out of something like this. We're grownups. We always used to say grownups could work out anything if they tried—if they really gave it their best shot. Didn't we say that? We can talk with each other—all those conversations on red-eyes and over dinners. I love to talk with you. Remember Seattle—the place with the great crab cakes? Remember how late we stayed up?

ACE (*sits at the table and looks at LEE full face, acknowledging the good memory*). I remember. You admitted how much of a liberal you really are. How could I forget?

LEE. Well, I was equally surprised when you told me how much of a liberal you are and the people you vote for. I didn't expect it. (*Teasing.*) You don't look like a lefty.

ACE (*smiles*). That's a little extreme.

LEE. Maybe, but we agree on things. We always agree, don't we?

ACE (*with real affection*). Well, we do, actually, sure. I enjoy talking with you as much as you enjoy talking with me.

LEE (*sits opposite ACE at the table*). And we're a good team when we work together.

ACE. Yeah, we're good. I like to take you to meetings with me. We do well.

LEE. And you help me. When I don't know what to do, you help me. You're there.

ACE. Friends help friends. You help me. When Bobby was in the hospital...

LEE. Poor little kid.

ACE. You were a good friend to me and Ellen. You were just fine. Ellen loves you. Bobby loves you.

LEE. And my family adores you. Uncle Ace.

ACE. Your kids are great.

LEE. Stephanie likes you better than any of her real uncles. She is just crazy about you.

ACE. Hey, she knows me so long she could be my own kid.

LEE. The game you gave her—we can't get her away from the computer.

ACE. I know what she likes.

LEE. It's like one family. One big family full of love.

ACE. So you love me.

LEE. As far as I'm concerned, you're my brother.

ACE. Yes.

LEE. Close. We are close.

ACE. So what would you do for a brother?

LEE. Anything.

ACE. Then I'll ask you to do something for me.

LEE. Name it. You want money, you've got it. You want help in your yard, you've got it. You want to take my boat for a week, sail away. For a month. Take a month's vacation.

ACE (*reaches across the table and puts his hand on LEE's arm*). Go to the senior vice president and tell him that you were totally full of crap, and he should have the note in my file removed.

LEE (*on his feet*). Whoooa, wait a minute. Just a minute.

ACE. Simply go and tell the man the truth.

LEE. Ah, Ace, I don't... I'd be telling him I misspoke.

ACE. Yes, you misspoke. Go and tell him that.

LEE. How could I do that? How could I go to a senior vice president and tell him that when I talk I don't know what I'm talking about? Would that help my future here?

ACE. I know it would be hard. I hate to ask, but it would be an effort to undo the damage you've done to my future.

LEE. You're asking a lot. I don't think I've done enough damage to turn around and put my future in the toilet.

ACE. You've done infinite damage.

LEE. No, it wasn't that bad.

ACE. I put my head on the pillow last night, and I saw that note. At three in the morning, I was still seeing that note. It says something about how I am suspected of having a drinking problem and have refused counseling. Do you think I am going anywhere in this organization? Do you think anything will come of the years I've put in? It's so bad. It is as bad as it could be. You tell a couple of stories to get close to a vice president, to amuse him, to get a laugh, and I am fucked forever. Don't tell me it wasn't that bad. I could kill you, I'm so angry. I could bash your stupid, fucking head in. *(ACE gets up and returns to his desk, concentrating again on the papers there.)*

LEE. You don't understand what happened. If you did, you wouldn't be so mad.

ACE *(swivels his chair to turn full face to LEE)*. Look, if you won't go upstairs to straighten this out, I'll do something else.

LEE. What?

ACE. I have to do something. All night, I tried to figure out the options. If you won't help, they're all risky.

LEE. What you have to understand is that I was talking out of regard for you. It was a kind of bragging in a way. He was asking about our numbers—why we do so well—why we're such a great team. I was telling him why we work well together. I said it was because we can play together, because we can get things lightened up, and the clients feel it, and they enjoy it and want to do business with us. He asked about the good times. I told some stories.

ACE. You told about San Diego.

LEE. It was very strange the way that happened.

ACE. That's the only time I've had too much to drink since we began traveling together. Lee, why did you tell about that?

LEE. It's so funny, and he's a nice guy ...

ACE. He's not a nice guy. He called Human Resources and told them to offer me counseling, without checking it out, without having evidence of any kind or giving me a chance to explain. He's not a good person or a good manager.

LEE. He seemed like a sweet, regular guy. For dinner that night, he told us to wear casual clothes. He wore jeans. It was so relaxed I forgot to be afraid of him. And the last thing I'd have thought was that he'd be negative about someone else's drinking; he was putting it away pretty good.

ACE. Lee, how did you do this? You're much too smart. You're too loyal, too close. What happened? Can you tell me?

LEE. Well, see, he liked my stories.

ACE. You can be very funny.

LEE. He laughed and laughed and asked for more. You sort of had to be there...the feeling of getting attention from a guy like that.

ACE. Um.

LEE. You get a lot of attention around here. Right then, I was getting some.

ACE. And basking in it.

LEE. Yes, it felt good, Ace—like something I deserve.

ACE *(with real concern)*. Do I take too much credit for your work?

LEE. I don't think... No, you really don't.

ACE. Perhaps I do.

LEE. No, really, no.

ACE. I've been moving in the organization. There are maybe five people who aren't so happy about that. Perhaps they would like to stop me. One of them brought in this guy.

LEE. No one can stop you. You're Ace. Your results are incredible. Everyone knows where you're going.

ACE. Where do you think I can go with that note in my file? I'm fucked. You told San Diego, and I'm truly fucked. How could you tell San Diego? To anyone? That was between us. That was sacred ground.

LEE. All I said was we went to a party.

ACE. Don't lie to me; Debra heard you. You said I got naked.

LEE. I said you did a little...

ACE. ...hokey-pokey, stark naked with a lipstick daisy on my ass. Right? You said that, right?

LEE. I could cut out my tongue. Okay? I could just cut it out of my head. I shouldn't have told it. While I was telling it, I was saying to myself, "Stupid, you shouldn't be telling this." I don't know what happened. He asked questions. He pushed. I kept talking. It spilled.

ACE. Yeah.

LEE. You're right. I'm a piece of shit.

ACE. So go tell the guy you created a wrong impression; in four years with me on the road, San Diego was the only time you ever saw me drink too much. All the other good times were only because I like good times.

LEE. I see what you mean.

ACE. Good, Lee, good.

LEE. But, ah, I'm sorry, I just can't fall on my sword that way.

ACE. You owe it to me.

LEE. Forgive me. Everyone spills a little when they shouldn't; everyone makes a misstep on sacred ground once in a while.

ACE. I've been in shock about this since they called. What to do? I was so hurt and furious, I just froze. But I can't leave it the way it is. You know I can't.

LEE. I apologize to you. Please, let's go on from here. Next week, in Denver, we'll have a good time. Maybe there'll be a chance to get into the mountains.

ACE. I could speak with him myself. I could ask for a meeting and make my case.

LEE. Him?

ACE. The senior vice president.

LEE. The kind of guy he is, he'd hate all the emotion.

ACE. Yeah, well, maybe I should speak with his boss.

LEE. What?

ACE. It's an option. It would be risky, though, bringing something of this nature so high.

LEE. You'd go to Carter? You'd do that? No!

ACE. Carter and I have been at the same functions for years. He knows me. He knows what I drink and what I don't drink, how I behave and how I don't behave. I'll tell him the whole story.

LEE. What whole story?

ACE. It's a story about how your mouth is out of control.

LEE. You go and say that about me to Carter, and I'm fucked.

ACE. Loose lips are not an asset in an organization. You were fucked when you told the story. You got some laughs, but it's not likely your big mouth won respect for you.

LEE. Ace, what are you doing to me?

ACE. Get out of my office.

LEE. Ace ...

ACE. Please go now. (*He picks up the phone and punches three buttons for an extension.*)

LEE (*reaches to hit the phone button to disconnect the call*). No, don't call!

(*Their eyes lock. LEE withdraws his hand.*)

ACE (*on the phone*). Hi, Joan, it's Ace. Does Archie have a minute or two to see me today? Yeah, I'll hold.

LEE. Archie? You call him Archie? You call Carter Archie? To his face? You call him Archie to his face? You call that woman Joan?

ACE. Hey, I'm Ace. I call Archie's boss Buzz.

LEE. The guy's name is Barney.

ACE. His baby brother couldn't say Barney. Buzz stuck. *(Into the phone.)* Yes, I can come now. Thanks. *(He hangs up. He starts to go off, holding his jacket.)*

LEE *(trying to stop ACE).* Don't do this! Ace, please...

ACE *(keeps going).* Get out of my way.

LEE. Stop! I'll do it! I'll go to the senior vice president. I'll do it.

ACE *(stops).* That would be better. I'd rather not bring other people into this. That's a good decision.

LEE. Okay. So let's finish our analyses, and get them in on time, and see the guy tomorrow. I haven't even started mine.

ACE. Let's see the guy now, if he can do it.

LEE. Now? All right, okay. The two of us—we'll make the case together, as members of a business team and friends. He'll have to listen. We do everything well together, and we'll do this well. We'll say there was a wrong impression. It was inadvertent. A misunderstanding. That's not so bad.

ACE *(picks up the phone, dials interoffice).* Hi, Joan. I had a little problem, and I've worked it out myself. Tell Archie thanks for the okay to come right up, but I won't need to do that now. Take care. *(He depresses the hook, releases it, looks at a phone list and dials interoffice.)* Hello, this is Ace Blackburn. I'd like to come upstairs with Lee Gardner for a few minutes, if your boss can see us. If he can't do it now, I'd like to make an appointment. Yes, I'll hold.

LEE. He's a busy guy—he's probably in a meeting or traveling. We won't get right in. Don't get your hopes up too much. It could be days, weeks.

ACE *(into the phone)*. Thanks very much. We'll be right up. *(Hangs up.)*

LEE. Now?

ACE. We'll stop at your office and get your jacket. *(ACE puts his jacket on.)*

LEE. We'll get it all straightened out. It'll be a relief. Next week, by the time we're in Denver, things will be back to normal. This'll just be one of those unfortunate incidents. I betcha it'll be a story—The Note in the File story. Maybe someday we'll even laugh about it.

ACE. You're not going to Denver with me. I'm taking Malcolm.

LEE. Because...?

ACE. Because he's smart. Because he's from Denver and has good contacts there, and because you're a pile of shit.

LEE. I'm going upstairs with you! It'll be fixed and forgiven. We'll be friends again.

ACE. Fixed. It'll be fixed. Maybe. Who knows? If it is fixed, I'll still know what you did. I'll always know. Can we go now, please? *(ACE starts out.)*

LEE *(hangs back)*. Ace, listen. You still don't understand.

ACE *(stops)*. Are you coming with me?

LEE. If you won't forgive, if you'll never forgive, I don't know.

ACE. All right. *(ACE starts out.)*

LEE. What will you say?

ACE *(stops)*. Whatever needs to be said to make things right again for me in this organization.

LEE. I'd better be there.

ACE. I would be if I were you.

LEE. Okay. All right. I'll come. I'll tell him. I'll explain the whole thing. I'll do it, Ace.

(They both start out, then ACE turns back.)

ACE. Thank you.
LEE. You'll understand sometime. You will.
ACE. Let's go.
LEE. I know you will. I just know it.

(Before he exits, ACE turns around and looks at LEE for a second or two, regretting that this ever happened. Then they are both gone in a quick blackout.)

END OF PLAY

CABBAGE HEAD

By
Julie Jensen

Cabbage Head is part of a larger work entitled **White Money**, winner of the Kennedy Center Award for New American Plays and workshopped at Shenandoah Playwrights Retreat. **White Money** has been produced by Salt Lake Acting Company, Actors Theatre of San Francisco, Mill Mountain Theatre in Roanoke, Va., the Source Theatre in Washington, D.C., and the Split Image Theatre in Baltimore.

CHARACTERS

ELLA: A woman in her 30s, pretty and worn, no one's fool.

MOTHER: A woman in her 60s, a religious fanatic, who may be hard of hearing.

SETTING: The front yard and interior of a trailer home.
TIME: The present.

CABBAGE HEAD

AT THE CURTAIN: *ELLA is discovered sitting in the yard of her mother's trailer. MOTHER is in a Lazy-Boy recliner in front of a television, a head of cabbage in her lap.*

ELLA *(to audience).* I'm hitchhiking along the Interstate 15. Illegal as hell. Have to watch out for the police. They pick you up and haul you in for something like that. But I don't get caught. Instead, I get a ride with this guy driving a sixteen-foot U-Haul on his way to Oklahoma. He wants to go to bed with me. I tell him, fine, go right ahead, I'm on my way home to commit suicide anyway. That seems to cool him off. He takes me as far as the Phillips 66 station in Panaca, Nevada. Now Panaca, Nevada, is another town a lot like Wendover, Nevada. It's good for hiding out in, not too good for much else. My mother lives there. In a trailer park west of town. I ain't seen her in years. So I bum a dime off the U-Haul guy and give her a call.

(ELLA enters MOTHER's trailer, surveys it.)

MOTHER. You gonna do what now?
ELLA. Well, I'm gonna get a job someplace, I guess.
MOTHER. Not here, you ain't.
ELLA. What's wrong with here?
MOTHER. Ain't no jobs in this town. Ain't no room in this house.

ELLA (*moving around the room, examining objects*). She's laid out on a Lazy-Boy watching TV. Reverend Winterose is on. Both her skin and the Naugahyde on the chair is the same color. I ain't moving back here, I says. You don't need to worry about that. She looks at me like she's relieved or else mad. Then goes back to the TV. Reverend Winterose is bawling and crying. Them are real tears, she says.

MOTHER. Reverend Winterose cries real tears.

ELLA. What else would he cry?

MOTHER. What I mean, they ain't no tricks with him. He cries, you can bet it's real tears.

ELLA. Lots of people can cry.

MOTHER. But not real tears.

ELLA. What other kind of tears are there? Television tears, she says.

MOTHER. Fake tears, Hollywood tears, television tears.

ELLA. She's eating from a head of cabbage in her lap. What happened to that old guy you used to live with, I say. What was his name?

MOTHER. Daddy.

ELLA. Oh, yeah. What happened to him?

MOTHER. He's out in the backyard.

ELLA. I check the window. Sure enough, there's the old guy out there sitting in the kiddie swing. What's he doing out there, I say.

MOTHER. He's being punished.

ELLA. He's being punished? Listen here, you ain't got his fingers taped to the chains, have you?

MOTHER. I got his fingers taped to the chains. He's being punished.

ELLA. That's what you used to do to me.

MOTHER. He's being punished. He don't like Reverend Winterose.

ELLA. A man after my own heart, I say. She just looks at me, then back at the TV.

MOTHER. He ain't ever been worth a damn.

ELLA. I know, Ma, but he don't deserve torture.

MOTHER. It ain't torture. It's punishment. Reverend Winterose makes him cry.

ELLA. And aren't they real tears? She looks at me again, then back at the TV. Nothing you do can make me laugh, she says.

MOTHER. Listen up.

ELLA. Yeah.

MOTHER. Nothing you say can make me laugh.

(ELLA moves to the fridge and opens it.)

ELLA. I decide to get off the subject for a while. I look in the fridge for something to eat. There's five heads of cabbage, a quart of Miracle Whip, and some colored Easter eggs, left over from when I was a kid. You know you're gonna lose your mind you set in front of that television long enough, I say. Steal your mind right out from under you. Not with Reverend Winterose, she says.

MOTHER. Not with Reverend Winterose. He's got the news.

ELLA. What news is that?

MOTHER. The good news. The right news.

(ELLA closes the fridge and explores the cupboards.)

ELLA. I'm going through the cupboards trying to find a can of tuna. Reverend Winterose is in tears again about the outpouring of love gifts. The tears are running down his face and onto the Bible in his hands. I asked for a chance, he cries, and you gave me a chance. I asked for an outpouring of the spirit, and you gave me an outpouring of the spirit. What's he bawling about, Ma, I say.

MOTHER. He's thankful.

ELLA. Thankful for what?

MOTHER. The outpouring of the spirit.

ELLA. And what's that mean?

MOTHER. He's rich.

ELLA. He's crying 'cuz he's rich?

MOTHER. He's crying 'cuz he's rich enough to be president.

ELLA. That's rich, I say. And I find a can of tuna. I'm stirring up something tasty. But she don't want any. Listen to me, Ma, I say.

MOTHER. I ain't listening to you.

ELLA. I'm talking as I'm stirring. You gotta get that old guy out of the sun.

MOTHER. What's it gonna do, dry up his brains? *(MOTHER laughs hysterically.)*

ELLA. She laughs. I don't. They get you for murder, you leave that old man taped out there in this heat.

MOTHER. He don't stay out there all day. I put him up under the trailer at midday. It's shady under there, he catches a breeze.

ELLA. Reverend Winterose is through crying now. He's dead serious. He's asking for something. Wants a daily love gift, he says, on the daily giving plan. Who wouldn't, I say. Who wouldn't want a daily love gift on the daily giving plan.

MOTHER. I'm on the daily giving plan.

ELLA. You give the man a daily gift of love?

MOTHER. I give a daily gift of love.

ELLA. On the daily giving plan?

MOTHER. On the daily giving plan.

ELLA. Sounds like you're sleeping with him, Ma.

MOTHER. Don't be silly.

(ELLA is stirring up the tuna.)

ELLA. Reverend Winterose has fat jowls and a little rose-bud mouth. Is that what you like about him, Ma, that little rosebud mouth? Like kissing a little goldfish? You think you're damned funny, she says.

MOTHER. You think you're so damned funny.

ELLA. How much money do you give him every day?

MOTHER. It's for the money-seeking vortex.

ELLA. Money-seeking vortex. Sounds dirty to me.

MOTHER. God wants us to be rich.

ELLA. I agree with you, Ma. But you're not. Reverend Winterose is the only one who is.

MOTHER. Through him I am rich. He cries real tears.

(ELLA finishes making a sandwich.)

ELLA. I'm whipping up a tuna salad san. You want a bite of this, I say.

MOTHER. No. I'm eating cabbage.

ELLA. Cabbage. That's all?

MOTHER. Yes. Cabbage.

ELLA. Cabbage for Christ, she says, and raises the cabbage head on high.

MOTHER. Cabbage for Christ.

ELLA. What the hell does that mean?

MOTHER. Just what it says.

ELLA. Ma, you gotta do something 'sides eat cabbage, lay yourself out on the Lazy-Boy, and watch Reverend Winterose. No, I don't, she says.

MOTHER. What more is there?

ELLA. Well, you could take care of that old guy you live with. She takes a bite of her cabbage. Reverend Winterose is calling out for action now. It's the hour of devil rebuking. Rebuke the devil in your life, he cries. Rebuke the devil in your house. Rebuke the devil in your body. Wherever the devil is, rebuke him now. My mother's laying out on the Lazy-Boy, with her arm raised, twitching and writhing. Is that the rebuking posture, I ask. Be still, she says. And she continues to writhe and twitch. Who you rebuking, Ma?

MOTHER. The devil in this house. The devil in the yard.

ELLA. Take a damn good look at that TV.

MOTHER. Be careful I don't rebuke you.

ELLA. She's writhing and twitching. That which causes pain and dissension, he says, that which causes disagreements and confusion, rebuke it in the name of Jesus. Rebuke! Rebuke! Each time he says the word rebuke, my mother lunges in the Lazy-Boy. Rebuke the television, I say. Bless the television, she says.

MOTHER. I bless the television set. Rebuke the devil.

ELLA. Rebuke that crazy bugger you watch.

MOTHER. I bless Reverend Winterose. I rebuke the devil.

ELLA. Reverend Winterose is bawling and gagging. His face is scarlet and swollen. My mother looks like she's in the middle of a grand mal seizure. I go to the fridge, take a cabbage from the shelf. She's yelling in tongues, so is Reverend Winterose. They sound like a couple of children playing Indians around a campfire. I stand behind my mother's chair, holding the cabbage, and the next time Reverend Winterose says the word rebuke, I throw the cabbage. *(ELLA pitches the cabbage through the television screen. The television explodes and goes silent. ELLA looks down at her mother.)* My mother relaxes like a person after electrocution. I take the head of cabbage from her lap and walk out the door. *(ELLA picks up the head of cabbage, then walks out the door.)* On my way through the yard, I untape the old guy's fingers and put him up under the trailer in the shade. And I roll the head of cabbage up under there with him. Then head on out for I don't know where. Las Vegas, I guess.

(ELLA shrugs and exits. Lights dim.)

END OF PLAY

THE NINE-VOLT TIME MACHINE

By
Richard Strand

The Nine-Volt Time Machine was originally produced in 1992 by American Blues Theatre in Chicago as part of "Monsters II: Visiting Hours." The play featured Stacey Guastaferro, Paul Quinn and Scott Anderson, and was directed by Andrea Dymond.

CHARACTERS

GINGER: A woman in her 40s who misses the Sixties. She is calm and meditative.
DRIP: A drip.
BILL: Ginger's husband.
VOICE (offstage)

SETTING: Chicago. Bare stage, minimum props: New Year's Eve party, bedroom, the Chicago River channel.

TIME: The present.

THE NINE-VOLT TIME MACHINE

AT THE CURTAIN: *GINGER holds a nine-volt battery and addresses the AUDIENCE.*

GINGER *(holds up a nine-volt battery).* This is a tine machine. It works by sticking the leads on your tongue. *(She sticks out her tongue and places the battery, leads down, on her tongue.)* Ow! Shit! *(She abruptly grabs her wrist and realizes she is not wearing a watch.)* Oh my God, what time is it?! *(She relaxes after she thinks about it.)* Actually, I guess I don't care. The question is mostly irrelevant. To me, anyway. *(Pause.)* Time travel makes you see things in a different light. It is, believe me, not like you think it is.

(Lights change and GINGER steps into the scene. A DRIP is sitting in a barstool, drunk and oblivious.)

GINGER. So here is what happened. I was tending bar at a New Year's Eve party on top of the John Hancock building and I was cornered by a drip who told me...

DRIP. You're much prettier than any of my ex-wives.

GINGER. Someone across the room shouted...

VOICE. Thirty minutes to midnight!

GINGER. "My husband should be here any minute," I said, hoping the drip would take a hint.

DRIP. You know, my last wife never did learn to make a decent soft-boiled egg.

GINGER. "I can't really talk right now," I said, trying to be rude. "I'm working." But there was no stopping him.

DRIP. Three-minute egg is a misnomer. People think you're supposed to boil 'em for three minutes. And that's too long.

GINGER (to the DRIP). You know, I'm really not interested in what you're saying.

DRIP. Here's what you do. You put the egg in cold water. Gotta be cold. Then you heat the water to boiling.

GINGER (to the DRIP). Stop talking, will you? I'm not listening.

DRIP. Then, as soon as the water's boiling, you yank the pan off the stove and let those eggs set for exactly two minutes and twenty seconds.

GINGER (to the DRIP). Shut up, will you? You bore me.

DRIP. And as soon as two minutes and twenty seconds is up, dunk those babies in cold water. That stops 'em from cooking anymore. That's all there is to it. That's how you make a soft-boiled egg.

GINGER. "Excuse me," I said. "I'm going to jump off the observation deck."

DRIP. Sure, honey, I'll be waiting for you.

GINGER. I grabbed my umbrella—there had been some threat of rain—and walked out on the observation deck. I wasn't really going to jump. At least, I don't think I was. (Pause.) Huh. Anyway, while I had hold of the metal railing, lightning struck the twin radio towers behind me. I felt electricity throughout my body. I was thrown back into the bar through an open door. Really thrown. I must have been airborne for thirty feet. I sailed through the air, my arms and legs flailing, over the heads of New Year's revelers, leaving behind me, if my recollection can be trusted, a trail of smoke. I landed, on my ass, behind the bar. After a brief rest, I lifted myself up and peeked over the bar, expecting an entire room full of partyers to be staring at me. No one was staring at me. No one was even looking at me, except the drip who was sitting in the same place he had been all evening. I tried to ask him, "What just happened?" but I couldn't make any words come out. And he said ...

DRIP. You're much prettier than any of my ex-wives.

VOICE. Thirty minutes to midnight.

GINGER. "My husband should be here any minute," I said, but the words were involuntary.

DRIP. You know, my last wife never did learn to make a decent soft-boiled egg.

GINGER. "Hey," I said, breaking myself out of the pattern, "I think I just traveled backwards in time."

DRIP. Three-minute egg is a misnomer. People think you're supposed to boil 'em for three minutes. And that's too long.

GINGER (to the DRIP). Did you hear me? I just traveled backward in time! I'm a time traveler.

DRIP. Here's what you do. You put the egg in cold water. Gotta be cold. Then you heat the water to boiling.

GINGER (to the DRIP). Stop talking! I'm trying to tell you something amazing.

DRIP. Then, as soon as the water's boiling, you yank the pan off the stove and let those eggs set for exactly two minutes and twenty seconds.

GINGER (to the DRIP). Shut up, will you? I've just had the most extraordinary experience of my life.

DRIP. And as soon as two minutes and twenty seconds is up, dunk those babies in cold water. That stops 'em from cooking anymore. That's all there is to it. That's how you make a soft-boiled egg.

GINGER. I'm a time traveler. I'm a goddamned time traveler.

DRIP. Sure, honey, I'll be waiting for you.

GINGER *(screaming, at the DRIP)*. I'VE JUST COME FROM THE FUTURE! I WAS ON THE OBSERVATION DECK WHEN LIGHTNING STRUCK! IT'S FIVE MINUTES EARLIER THAN IT USED TO BE. I'VE ALREADY LIVED THIS PART OF MY LIFE! I HAVE GONE BACK IN TIME! *(To AUDIENCE.)* And then, suddenly, I knew from the silence that, for the first time this evening, the drip had heard me. And so had everyone else at the party. The band quit playing. Everyone quit dancing. All eyes were on me: the nut who thought she could travel through time. And the drip said...

DRIP. Listen, babe. Here's five. I think my wife just came in.

GINGER. ... and he left me alone for the rest of the night. Pretty much everyone left me alone all night. I was pretty sure that this was not something I was going to be able to discuss with just anyone.

(Lights change. GINGER steps out of the scene with the DRIP and into the scene with BILL.)

GINGER. I tried to bring up my time traveling to my husband, Bill. He was grumpy, as usual. I don't think he really heard me. He said...

BILL. Whatever makes you happy.

GINGER. ...and went back to sleep. I woke him up an hour later and I was insistent. *(To BILL.)* Bill, we have to talk. We have to. I traveled in time. I did.

BILL. No, you didn't.

GINGER. Yes, I did.

BILL. Time travel is impossible. Carl Sagan said so.

GINGER. But, Bill...

BILL. If you went back in time you could change the future. You could go back and destroy your time machine. So then you wouldn't be able to travel back in time. Only you already did. So you got an unresolvable paradox. Unless, of course, it's impossible to travel back in time in the first place—which it is—so why don't you turn off the light and let me sleep?

GINGER. But it doesn't work like that. Everything happens the same way it...

BILL. Say you went into the future. And, on the very site you put your time machine, somebody built a house. You'd materialize inside a wall and be killed instantly. Forget it. It's impossible. Now turn off the light.

GINGER. I didn't go into the future. I went into the past. I was at the top of the Hancock...

BILL. Say you're at the top of the Hancock. You go back in time to 1940. The Hancock hasn't even been built. You'd fall one hundred stories and be killed. It's impossible. Now please—please—let me go back to sleep.

GINGER. I did. It happened. I went back in time last night.

BILL. Well, for your own safety, don't do it again. Now turn off the light.

GINGER. I tried to turn off the light. But the wiring in our house has always been bad. I felt a jolt as I touched the switch. Nothing more; just a jolt. And then I heard Bill say...

BILL. Time travel is impossible. Carl Sagan said so.

GINGER. Bill, it's happened again. I've gone back in time again.

BILL. If you went back in time you could change the future. You could go back and destroy your time machine. so then you wouldn't be able to travel back in time. Only you already did...

GINGER.	BILL.
And Bill droned on, exactly as he had before. He had said this once and would have to say it again. Unless I could figure a way to stop him. I tried screaming. (Screaming.) Aaaaaaaaa! (Pause.) Bill showed no signs of having heard me scream. He just kept blabbing away, like he was an expert on time travel. Like most men, Bill was an expert on almost everything. I tried covering his mouth with my hand. (GINGER covers BILL's mouth with her hand.) I had muffled the sound a little, but Bill seemed unaware of the hand covering his mouth. He felt rigid—like steel—there would be no simple way to stop him. I would simply have to wait for him to run down. (GINGER lets go of BILL's mouth.)	So you got an unresolvable paradox. Unless, of course, it's impossible to travel back in time in the first place— which it is—so why don't you turn off the light and let me sleep? (Pause.) Say you went into the future. And, on the very site you put your time machine, somebody built a house. You'd materialize inside a wall and be killed instantly. Forget it. It's impossible. Now turn off the light. (Pause.) Say you're at the top of the Hancock. You go back in time to 1940. The Hancock hasn't even been built. You'd fall one hundred stories and be killed. It's impossible. Now please— please—let me go back to sleep.

GINGER. Bill, I'm stuck. I can't move. I'm trapped.

BILL. Well, for your own safety, don't do it again. Now turn off the light.

GINGER. My hand fell, hitting the switch, and I was back in my own time again.

(Lights change and GINGER steps out of the scene.)

GINGER. My first experience with time travel was the result of a bizarre sequence of events and an electrical shock that might have killed me. The second experience was the result of a minor shock—a shock which I probably wouldn't even have noticed if it weren't for the five-minute lurch backwards in time. So I figured that the first jolt had made me, well, time-travel prone and that now any electrical shock was apt to send me backwards. And sure enough, experiments with an open light socket and a watch confirmed that I could travel backward at will. Almost any jolt would send me backwards a few minutes. But I was unable to alter the past. Or my present. Or, it seemed, my future. I was always drawn back to the point of my departure. And I would remain there until my past rejoined my present. I resolved to find a way to not be drawn back to the point of departure. I was determined to find a way to alter my past. And here is what I did.

I drove my car to the Chicago River—actually to the channel they built to reverse the flow—and I sat by the bank for an hour or so. Then, at high noon, I took out my nine-volt battery, stuck out my tongue and licked it. It hurts, but not much. I checked my watch again; it was three minutes before noon. Quickly, while I seemed to have freedom of choice, I ran to the river and jumped in. I let the current carry me. And I started swimming, with the current, trying to get as far downstream as I could before I felt the draw to return to my point of departure. I'm not a very good swimmer—it did occur to me that I might drown—but the current was strong and I managed to keep my head above water.

Then I felt the draw. There is no fighting it once you feel it. I managed to get a look at my watch—it was about a minute to noon. And, involuntarily, I began swimming upstream. I was a far stronger swimmer than I had been—than I had ever been in my life—and the current seemed not to be slowing me down. I was swallowing water. I was nearly unable to breathe. And I considered that, if nothing else, dying would certainly alter my path. But I thought maybe the current was slowing me down a little—just enough, maybe—to make me late for my date with the present time.

As I rounded the bend, to my amazement, I saw myself sitting on the bank. I saw myself take a nine-volt battery and prepare to lick it. And yet I was still in the middle of the river, swimming upstream, watching a drier version of myself head for the bank. There were two of me now. I'm sorry to use an old cliché, but the fact of the matter is, I was in over my head.

Before I—you know, the other I—the dry one—was able to jump in the river, I shouted to me. "Hey!" I said. "Don't do it! This could get out of hand!"

The dry me stared at me in utter amazement. I was in no way prepared for what I saw. Neither, I suppose, was I. If you follow.

(GINGER assumes two personae.)

GINGER. Who the hell are you?

WET GINGER. I wasn't sure I cared for my attitude. And I told me so. *(To GINGER.)* Take a 'lude. I'm you. Only I'm the first you. The original you. You are sort of a copy of me.

GINGER. Well, I could see the wet bitch was me, but I wasn't sure I cared for my attitude and I told me so. *(To WET GINGER.)* Who says I'm the copy? I say you're the copy.

WET GINGER *(to AUDIENCE)*. Well that's just stupid. Obviously I was here first and that makes me the original. And I told me so. *(To GINGER.)* Look, I was here first.

GINGER. She was here first. That's a laugh. I've been here since eleven a.m., tubby.

WET GINGER. Tubby?! *(To AUDIENCE.)* I need this from me? *(To GINGER.)* If it weren't for the fact that you're me ...

GINGER. Yeah? What? You'd do what, fat girl?

WET GINGER. Well, I was so pissed at me by that time that I let me have it right across the mouth. *(She slaps herself.)* And I felt bad almost instantly. I hated me. Both of me. And I wanted me to hit me back, hard. But rather than hitting me back, the dry bitch started walking, crying. *(To GINGER.)* Hey, what are you doing?

Don't cry. I hate it when we cry. What are we crying for?

GINGER. We hate our life. *(She takes out the nine-volt battery.)*

WET GINGER. I know. I know we do. But, uh, we're going to change that. I mean, who says we gotta be married to a jerk and work at the Hancock? Huh? Who says? *(GINGER is preparing to lick the battery.)* Look, don't do that! We can change our lives. We can! We can be friends. We can be roommates! Don't lick the battery!

GINGER. I don't think I have a choice.

WET GINGER. And she licked her nine-volt battery... *(GINGER licks the leads.)* ...and I disappeared. *(GINGER disappears.)* You have no idea what that feels like.

GINGER *(as her regular self again)*. Well, that's pretty much everything that has happened so far. Except, I figured that with two of me, the other me could go back and live with Bill. I moved out to the 'burbs. I live alone. I'm writing *haiku*. I'm happier now. And I avoid electricity and other wonders of the modern world. I keep this battery as a memento of my former life. It is no longer charged. It has lost its ability to act as a time machine. I can touch it to my tongue with impunity. *(She sticks out her tongue and touches it with the leads of the battery.)* Ow! Shit! *(She abruptly grabs her wrist and realizes she is not wearing a watch.)* Oh my God, what time is it?!

(The lights fade to black.)

END OF PLAY

THE TURNOVER

By
Adam Kraar

The Turnover was written for Primary Stages' "Urban Myths Project," where it was given a reading in 1995. It was a finalist for the Actors Theatre of Louisville Ten-Minute Play Contest in 1996, and had a workshop production at the New York State Theatre Institute in 1998. It premiered in 1998 at Todo Con Nada in New York City.

CHARACTERS

VINNIE: 28. An introverted dreamer and loner.
MARY: 26. Though people think she's slightly retarded, she's essentially just a child-like soul.

SETTING: The rooftop of a brownstone in Brooklyn. There is a typewriter on a typing table with a clip-on light, and a chair.

TIME: The present, summer, after dark.

THE TURNOVER

AT THE CURTAIN: *VINNIE is alone on the roof, seated at the desk. He types one letter, then becomes lost in thought, subconsciously touching his lower lip with his fingers. After a few moments, MARY enters quietly, carrying a paper bag. She comes up behind VINNIE and watches him.*

MARY. ...What are you doing?

VINNIE *(startled)*. Huh!? —*Mary!*

MARY. Sorry. Sorry.

VINNIE. What the f—? —What are you doing?

MARY. Sorry.

VINNIE. How did you get up here?

MARY. I went to my roof, then went over Catapano's roof, then Sannuto's—

VINNIE. How'd you know I was up here? Have you been following me?

MARY. It's cool up here!

VINNIE. Mary, what did I tell you?

MARY. I made you something. Apple. I put in cinnamon, raisins, brown sugar...

VINNIE. God, that looks good.

MARY. Eat it now.

VINNIE. Mary, you gotta leave me alone.

MARY. I put in a clove. I added a dash of salt, like you said.

VINNIE. Mary—

MARY *(of the typewriter)*. Is this yours?

VINNIE. Don't touch that. No one is allowed up here. It's very dangerous.

MARY. Nah.

VINNIE. Sometimes robbers come by here. They don't like the way you look, bing! They push you off the roof.

MARY. You could protect me.

VINNIE. I can't protect you anymore!

MARY. I'm not scared.

VINNIE. Well, you should be.

MARY. Why?

VINNIE. A robber might like the way you look. Might mess with you.

MARY. Mess with me? Like how?

VINNIE. You know. *(Beat.)* No one is allowed up here.

MARY. Johnny accidentally on purpose ... touches ...

VINNIE. What did he do?

MARY. It was an accident. Accidents can happen.

VINNIE. Son of a bitch, did he ... ? Tell me what he did.

MARY. He was just joking. He's got a girlfriend. Nancy. They're serious even though she's kinda stuck-up.

VINNIE. Mother of Jesus! What am I gonna do with you?

MARY *(both innocent and coy)*. I don't know.

VINNIE. I don't want you hanging around no more.

MARY. *Why?*

VINNIE. You keep tailing me, I'm never gonna talk to you again. Understand?

MARY. Is it 'cause Johnny touched me?

VINNIE. No! Only, if he tries anything you hit him hard with a bread tray and scream. Okay?

MARY. Then can we go watch the boats?

VINNIE. Look, Mary, we had a lot of great times together, watchin' the boats—

MARY. Shooting off Roman candles!

VINNIE. Right. But—

MARY. Shooting off bottle rockets! And then that time we ran from the cops?

VINNIE. Yeah, that was great, but—

MARY. Don't you want your hot apple turnover?

VINNIE. No. *(Beat.)* I do and I don't. Listen to me. I like you.

MARY. Aw, Vinnie...

VINNIE. But I can't hang out with you anymore. I got a novel to write.

MARY. *Romancing the Rom!* Unit 3765 falls in love with a human female. But it is forbidden.

VINNIE. ...I've got a girlfriend now. And when I'm not working on my novel or fixing VCRs or air-conditioners, I've gotta spend time with her.

MARY. You got a girlfriend?

VINNIE. What, is that so amazing?

MARY. Who?

VINNIE. You don't know her.

MARY. What's her name?

VINNIE. ...Felicia.

(Pause.)

MARY. We could still go see the boats? Why don't we go now? I know! We could sneak into the warehouse, like last week. It was cool in there. Like...another planet. Where anything could happen. A good planet. *(Beat.)* Didn't you think it was cool?

VINNIE. You're pretty, Mary. Beautiful. But it's like...not everybody likes strawberry ice cream. That's all.

MARY. You like strawberry. *(Beat.)* Hey, this turnover's getting cold. Try a bite.

(MARY holds it in front of his mouth, VINNIE takes a bite.)

VINNIE. ...Oh boy. That is delicious! Thank you.

MARY. The next bite, all apple.

VINNIE. Just put it...

MARY. Which chapter you doin'?

VINNIE. ...I'm just starting.

MARY. I know how to type. You wanna see? Lemme show you.

VINNIE. No.

MARY. Why not?

VINNIE. 'Cause I got work to do.

MARY. You weren't typing before.

VINNIE. That's 'cause I was thinking!

MARY. What were you thinking?

VINNIE. Mary!

(Pause.)

MARY. You really have a girlfriend?

(Pause.)

VINNIE. No. I mean, I've had women. I coulda had a lotta girlfriends, but I've made sacrifices for my art. —What, you think I'm lyin'?

MARY *(smiling)*. Yeah.

VINNIE *(waving it off)*. Ahhh—

MARY. I love the air up here. It's like a different...atmosphere. Do you like it?

VINNIE *(to himself)*. Ridiculous. Absolutely ridiculous.

MARY. What? *Tell me.*

VINNIE. You can't—ever—let people use you. Touch you. For a joke or...if they're not gonna be your boyfriend, if they just kiss you in the dark in some ware-

house and then around other people, pretend they don't
know you, that's no good—

MARY. I don't care.

VINNIE. You gotta care! You gotta start seeing, that you
are special. You think anyone else in the world can
make a turnover like that? No way! Only Mary. *(Beat.)*
You gotta get someone else to cut your hair.

MARY. My aunt does it.

VINNIE. No kidding. *(Slight pause. He touches her hair,
then pulls his hand away.)* It's not right. I know you
too many years.

MARY. Since the third grade. You were in fifth grade.
They were chasing me 'cause I used to never talk, they
caught me and twisted my arm. "Say something, stupid!" I wouldn't. Then you came and pulled 'em off.
And they never chased me again.

VINNIE. It wouldn't be right. For lots of reasons. So I
want you to leave, and not follow me around. We can
talk when you're at the bakery. Okay? Goodbye, Mary.

(MARY sits down at the typewriter and types.)

VINNIE. My God, you *do* type! "The quick brown fox
jumped over the lazy dog." That's excellent.

MARY. I could type your book.

VINNIE. Shit.

MARY. Tell me what to type.

(Pause.)

VINNIE. Here goes—ready? "Chapter Two... The 800 Mega-
byte Heart. Vyadec drove his shuttlecraft deep into space,
deeply disturbed..." *(MARY types efficiently, VINNIE
watches with amazement.)* Man, you're fast! "Could an

android really go for— *(Correcting himself.)* love a human female? ...Because...not only was it forbidden... "

MARY. By the Third Robotic Conference!

VINNIE. "...Vyadec knew what Jane Jiles of Delos Prime deserved was a human man...a fleshling...who could give her...his blood, and heart, and...illogical...devotion. It was impossible."

MARY. But...

VINNIE. Impossible.

MARY. The woman...gives Vyadec new subroutines!

VINNIE. No, it's burned into him. He can only look at her...as different than what he is.

MARY. She can change. She has a scientist install a CPU inside her heart.

VINNIE. The android would never allow that. She might think that's what she wants, but it would be wrong, and she'd end up regretting it.

MARY. Never!

(Beat. VINNIE grabs the paper out of the typewriter and pretends to read.)

MARY. What?

VINNIE. Uh, your spelling.

MARY. "V-y-a-d-e-c." Right?

VINNIE. Yes. —No. I'm sorry. It's just not gonna work.

MARY. You... You could teach me. ...Please?

VINNIE. Please, Mary. Just go. *(Instead, MARY closes her eyes and puckers her lips, inviting him to kiss her. Harshly:)* Get outta here!! You're holding me up! Damn! ...You better leave through my house, you'll break your neck. *(Ignoring this, MARY crosses over the roof.)* Mary! Wait! *(He has to grab her arm to keep her from going.)*

MARY. What?

VINNIE. You gotta understand. It has nothing to do with your spelling or anything about you.

MARY. You think I'm stupid!!

VINNIE. No! It's me. It's all me. *(He lets go of her arm.)* I have these plans— Well, ideas. I have these big ideas about Hollywood. And nobody around here belongs in Hollywood, right? *(He sees MARY's hurt expression.)* Hey. *(He grabs the turnover.)* Take a bite of this, just do it. *(MARY takes a bite of the turnover.)* Huh? Whoever made this turnover is like, the Einstein of pastry. *(He takes a bite.)* Mmmm!

MARY. ...You're goin' to Hollywood?

VINNIE. Aw hell, I haven't even written the damn thing yet. I love telling you about it. But when I sit down to type it...it...it just doesn't...matter. *(Beat.)* I'm sorry.

MARY. That's okay. Well, I gotta go.

VINNIE. Where you goin'?

MARY. Home.

VINNIE *(imitating the movie)*. E.T. go home. Hanh? *(He extends his finger á la E.T., but MARY doesn't respond.)* Come on. ...What is it?

MARY. It's stupid.

(He moves to her; she backs away.)

VINNIE. Mary... *(She stops but keeps her distance.)* I'm a lot like that android. Like, you know how Vyadec is 'sposed to be incapable of any emotion? But when he sees that girl on the Delosian moon, his CPU starts buzzing like crazy. He goes through all these changes, 'cause he's sure something is wrong with him. And, you know, he almost lets 'em reformat his whole CPU. He woulda been a blank slate, forgot all about her, spending eternity alone, looping through space. But then, at the last moment, he sees: He may not be a human being, but he can tell when a human woman is special... fascinating... and, incredibly...

(VINNIE touches her shoulder. She shyly looks away. Pause. VINNIE takes his hand away. Beat. MARY suddenly grabs him and they kiss ardently for five seconds.)

VINNIE. Wow.

(Slight pause.)

MARY *(suddenly)*. Vinnie, look!
VINNIE. A shooting star! Quick, make a wish.
MARY. I wish—
VINNIE. Don't tell me. If you tell me, it won't come true.

(MARY puts her hand over her mouth. She and VINNIE look at each other as the lights fade to black.)

END OF PLAY

RUSH TO JUDGMENT

By
Nancy Hanna

Rush to Judgment premiered at the Dallas Playwright's Project Annual Ten-Minute Play Festival at Frank's Place, Dallas Center Theatre, 1998. It was directed by Christopher Carlos and featured Deborah Kirby and Colleen A. O'Connor.

CHARACTERS

RUTH: Erin's mother.

ERIN: Upper 20s-30s. Ruth's single daughter, still living at home.

SETTING: The kitchen of a small Midwest house with an archway to the living room and a door to the backyard.

TIME: The present. A dangerous storm is approaching.

RUSH TO JUDGMENT

AT THE CURTAIN: *RUTH and ERIN are standing in the kitchen.*

RUTH. Jean doesn't believe it.

ERIN *(looking outside)*. I'm afraid.

RUTH. How could she sit all those years in church...be a hearer and a doer but not a believer?

ERIN *(crossing)*. Maybe we should turn on the radio.

RUTH. I mean, why bother?

ERIN. I'm gonna take all the pictures off the walls.

RUTH. I sat next to this woman for forty years. She's head of the pancake breakfast, for gosh sakes. Last year we sent fifteen packages of cookies off to our missionaries and college students. No one else showed up, just Jean and me did it.

ERIN. Mama, it's comin'. I know it is.

RUTH. I know it is too and that's what scares me. Jean's been my best friend since first grade, Mrs. Wiser's class. I'm gonna call the preacher. I've got to talk this over with someone. Figure out what to do. Maybe he can talk sense into her.

ERIN. Where's the tape? Mama, why's this radio not workin'?

RUTH. Batteries. *(To the phone.)* What's his number? I gotta look it up.

ERIN. Don't you have batteries somewhere? Masking tape for the windows. Mama, where's the masking tape?

RUTH. The years I've worshiped with this woman. She doesn't believe any of it, that's what she said. She doesn't believe in that "blood stuff." That's what she said. "Communion makes me want to choke," thinkin' she's eatin' flesh. "It's sick," she said. "All the killin' in the Old Testament. God makin' earth and all the stuff on it, in only six days." She doesn't believe it. Not one word of it.

ERIN. I found it. *(With tape, she begins to tape up the windows.)*

RUTH. Help me find it. Erin, I can't find the preacher's number. You'd think I'd know it after all this time.

ERIN. That's tellin'.

RUTH. What?

ERIN. Well, sometimes the brain blocks out information...subconsciously.

RUTH. What do you mean by that?

ERIN. You never wanted to learn his number.

RUTH. What's that have to do with anything? I know the man. I know where to reach him.

ERIN. How often do you call him? In a week? How often do you suppose you've got church business and you pick up the phone to call him?

RUTH. I don't have any idea.

ERIN. Oh yes, you do. Come on, think about it. You better go bring the dog in.

RUTH. You are some piece of work, aren't you? As if I'm not upset enough, you've got to heap on misery. *(Opens door and calls to their dog.)* Sassy! Sassy! Get in here. *(Back to ERIN.)* I find out my best friend is an a-gonostic and now you're tryin' to turn things in on me. Your hair is dirty. Why do I always have to remind you? For twenty years now, I have to remind you to wash your hair.

ERIN. I like it dirty.

RUTH. A storm's comin' and it might take the water out and you are going to go around after with your hair dirty. Go wash your hair. Right now. Before it gets here.

ERIN. That's a joke, right?

RUTH. No, I'm not kiddin'. Come on, right now. I'll help you, before the storm comes. It's like dyin' in a car accident with dirty underpants. *(Pushing ERIN toward the sink.)* Come on, let's just wash it in the sink.

ERIN. Don't do it, Mama. Don't you dare do it.

RUTH. You're going to feel so much better with clean hair.

(RUTH starts to wash ERIN's hair. ERIN yields to this.)

ERIN. Mama, not dishwasher soap.

RUTH. Just shut up.

ERIN. Do you have any canned foods?

RUTH *(scrubbing ERIN's hair)*. Um-hum. Lots. And some of Jean's canned peaches too.

ERIN. Do you have matches?

RUTH. Erin, don't ask me stupid questions.

ERIN. That feels good, Mama. You should have been a beautician.

RUTH. I could have been a lot of things.

ERIN. Think of all the women you could have ministered to in a beauty shop.

RUTH. 226-7352. 1 know it. I know, I know it.

ERIN. Women have to sit there and take pretty much anything their beautician has to give.

RUTH. 226-7358.

ERIN. And they never complain about a bad haircut...too afraid to hurt the hairdresser's feelings.

RUTH *(ends washing ERIN's hair, crosses to phone)*. Get a towel.

ERIN. They just switch beauty parlors, is all. Never go back to them again.

RUTH. Maybe if I act like I'm dialing it.

ERIN *(towel-drying hair)*. I knew Jean wasn't right.

RUTH *(dialing phone)*. 2-2-6-7-3, that's corner to corner. It's just the last two I'm not sure about...5-3.

ERIN. I've seen her roll her eyes one too many times. And then, there was no agreement. She never "Amened" anything. Not once. Even with those evangelists. Never a peep.

RUTH. Ah, hello. Is this Reverend Burns' residence? Oh, I'm sorry to bother you. Well, I'm so sorry. Goodbye, now. It's so close to that. *(Dialing again.)* 2-2-6-7-3-5—6.

ERIN *(looking out window)*. It's picking up. The porch furniture. We forgot the porch furniture. I'm going to go put it in the garage. *(Exits.)*

RUTH. Ah, yes, hello. Is this the Reverend Burns'? Yes, this is Ruth Meeks. Yes, I heard about that. We're just putting away our yard furniture. No kidding. Is that right? Who is this? Oh, Albert. Why yes, of course I know you, Albert...Ritter. Yes, I guess it's been about twenty years or so. I didn't even recognize your voice. How are you? How's your...corn coming in this year? Yes, I guess it is a little early. You think it's heading our way then? Well, I hope your fields aren't hit, Albert. No, I was just trying to reach Reverend Burns.

2-2-6-7-3-5-7. Now, I should have remembered that. Sevens on each end. Yes, we'll be careful. Thank you, Albert. No, we're...I'm fine. Don't you dare come over here. Not ever. *(Slams the phone down, shaken.)*

(ERIN re-enters.)

ERIN. It's not right out there.

RUTH. I got the number.

ERIN. We're in for it. Miss Stormy Weather's come to pay us a visit.

RUTH. Now how do you suppose a heathen like Albert Ritter knew the pastor's phone number. He's never graced the steps of a church door in his life.

(RUTH becomes "unglued." ERIN continues making preparations for the storm by filling the sink with water.)

RUTH. Albert knew the pastor's phone number. I can't even imagine it. Now what would those two possibly have to talk about? Dry your hair, Erin. You don't want to have wet hair when the storm hits. *(She sits ERIN down in a chair and towel-dries her hair.)* Are you ready, sweetie? If the storm hits and things go bad? I've lived every day like it was my last for years.

ERIN. Yes, I know. *(Takes hold of RUTH's hands on her head.)* You're trembling?

RUTH. If a board breaks loose and strikes open my head, so be it. I don't get it all, but I don't need to. Mystery is precious to me. Something our human minds ought not bother to sort through. Somebody ought to explain that to Jean.

ERIN. Like infinity? Eternity? Where it just goes on and on and on.

RUTH. Yes. And why some die young and others linger on past their use. Living's a flawed business. So's dyin'. So's love.

ERIN. Oh really? And what would you know about that? Maybe it's time you speak some pearls of wisdom about love to me, Mama... before our time runs out and the very last day is upon us.

RUTH. Are you bein' smart? There, how's that? *(Refers to hair.)* Almost all dried up.

ERIN. Thanks. Well, it's just if boards go flyin', I might never benefit from all your experience. So who was he? Before the boards fly, Mama, I'd like to know. I've heard so many versions I can't keep up. And seein' as this is likely the last day and all, I think it's time. Right here, right now. I can't get it out of anyone. Not even Jean. Maybe she's had enough of keepin' secrets. No more church, no more Ruth. The woman's makin' a clean sweep. Jean's all wore out. You and the church wore her out, Mama.

RUTH. That's not true, a person can't wear another person out.

ERIN. Why are you trembling?

RUTH. It's not like we're a pair of shoes or somethin'.

ERIN. Or in your case, a pair of orthopedic tennis shoes.

RUTH. I do not wear orthopedic shoes.

ERIN. Look down. Easy Spirits, only you're not.

RUTH. They're the most comfortable shoe you can buy. And you've got to take care of your feet... that's one part of your body that can wear out...

ERIN. I just want to know about the other half of my equation. Maybe that's why things haven't worked out so great for me. Look at me, Mama. I don't finish stuff. I couldn't even get through the teacher's-aid class at junior college. A storm is comin'. If one of us don't make it, say you for instance, who's gonna fill in the blanks?

RUTH. We all have blanks, spots that need filled. They're God reminders, places only he can fill up. That's why we pant like deer. It makes us thirsty for more understanding.

ERIN. Who was he? Who was my daddy? There's a spot needs fillin' and you're gonna fill it right now, so someday I can graduate from junior college and be a teacher's aid. I know it wasn't the immaculate conception. And I'm pretty sure, knowing you, it wasn't the immaculate "preconception." More like, the not-so-immaculate "misconception."

RUTH. Just shut your mouth, right now.

ERIN *(looking outside, then turning to RUTH, dangerously angry)*. What are you so afraid of? It's gettin' black out there. And I have to side with Jean on this one, call me an agnostic, I don't believe my daddy was an angel, and I don't think he was a devil either. This isn't a God "thing," Mama, this is a "you" thing. It's about you tellin' the truth, not heavenly mystery. *(She begins to shake RUTH.)* Tell me about love, Mama. I wouldn't know, would I? I'm the last remaining virgin from my class at Grover Plains High. No one's ever touched me that way. What's it like?

(RUTH slaps ERIN. Stunned, ERIN shoves RUTH to the floor, pinning RUTH's arms down and waving her wet hair in RUTH's face.)

ERIN. Give it up. Tell me once and for all. Who was it? Somebody from around here? A traveling salesman? An itinerant evangelist?

RUTH. Absolutely not. Now, stop it. *(Losing strength, defeated.)* Stop it, Erin, please.

ERIN. Here comes the storm to tear us all to pieces. Who was he?

RUTH. Albert. *(Beat.)* Now stop it and go brush your hair?

ERIN. Who?

RUTH. Albert Ritter.

ERIN. Albert Ritter, the guy you just dialed on the telephone?

RUTH. He got fresh with me on a high school hayride. He got me drunk with beer. And started kissing...I can't believe I'm tellin' you this.

ERIN. You called his number instead of the preacher? The heathen corn farmer, who lives a mile down the road, is my daddy?

RUTH. That's why my hands were shakin'. Hearin' his voice. Now can we just shut up about it.

ERIN. Or should I say sperm donor. You all are more sophisticated than I thought around here.

RUTH. Now, there you know. Let me up.

(They BOTH rise.)

ERIN. Well that's somethin'. You really spilled a good one. Now that wasn't so bad, was it? All the years, hidin' the simplest story...

RUTH. Those Ritters aren't worth two nickels to rub together. His father was the dumbest corn farmer in the county. Starved to death every cow they ever owned. They were poor as dirt. Now you can go finish your schooling. And please, go put a brush through your hair.

ERIN. Oh glory, here it comes. It's almost here. We better get to the bathroom.

RUTH. But it's all tangled. Doesn't that bother you?

ERIN. No!

RUTH. It will dry all tangled. And witchy.

ERIN. Come on, Mom. Let's go get in the bathtub.

RUTH. No, no, I'm stayin' right here. *(RUTH stands in the door archway.)*

ERIN. You're supposed to go to the bathroom... inside the house.

RUTH. The archway's fine. Come here, so I can kiss my girl. Baby, you're no Ritter, you're mine. And you can do anything you put your mind to. You're the smartest kid I know.

ERIN. The windows, if they blow out, we'll get all cut up.

RUTH. It doesn't matter.

ERIN *(looks out window)*. Here it comes, Mama. God Almighty. I see it. Come look. Maybe we oughtta get outta here.

RUTH. Come here, baby girl. So I can hold you. You're all mine. You have nothin' to do with anyone else.

ERIN. Don't you want to see how bad it is?

RUTH. No, I'm trustin' God. Come here, baby girl.

ERIN. I can't. I'm not like you. I haven't given up... in fact, I haven't even gotten started. *(She pulls the table offstage toward the bathroom.)* I'm gettin' in the tub and putting this table over top of me. Come—on—now—Mama. I mean it!

RUTH. I wonder where Jean is? I hope she's safe.

ERIN *(offstage)*. I'm in the tub. I have the hairbrush. Come on, Mama. You can come brush my hair.

RUTH. God's fury, headed right towards us. We're bein' judged.

ERIN. You can tell me about Albert. Livin' next to him all these years and never speaking.

RUTH. Or maybe it's old Slue Foot his self—tryin' to kill and destroy...

ERIN. What's the name of this storm? It's not called Albert, is it?

RUTH *(yelling at the storm)*. You can't touch me. You're not gettin' me and my girl.

ERIN. Now that would be I-ronic. I'm the livin', breathin' evidence how it's possible to make hay while the sun don't shine.

RUTH. Greater is He that is in me!

ERIN *(beat)*. I'm brushin' my hair, Mama, come and see.

RUTH *(squeezes eyes closed)*. 2-2-6-7-5-3-7, that's his number. *(Shouting.)* The pastor's number is 2-2-6-7-5-3-7. I knew it, Erin.

(Blackout.)

END OF PLAY

THE SIXTH FLOOR MUSEUM

By

Quincy Long

The Sixth Floor Museum was presented by the HB Playwrights Foundation and Theatre as one of "The Museum Plays: Eleven Short Plays in Two Evenings," New York City, 1998.

CHARACTERS

DUB and BELLE: Middle-aged couple, small-town visitors to Dallas.

LOU and PATTY: Middle-aged couple, once from Dub and Belle's hometown, now residents of Dallas.

SETTING: The Sixth Floor Museum, a national museum in Dallas, located on the sixth floor of the book depository from which Lee Harvey Oswald, according to all reliable evidence, fired the shots that killed President John F. Kennedy. Cardboard boxes stenciled "BOOKS" are piled around and in front of a partly open window.

TIME: The present.

THE SIXTH FLOOR MUSEUM

AT THE CURTAIN: *DUB and LOU enter. DUB is listening to a guided tour on headphones. The men stop and stare at the prime exhibit, a pile of cardboard boxes surrounding the partially open window from which Oswald fired his famous shots.*

DUB *(taking off headphones).* My God.

LOU. That's the spot.

DUB *(standing on tiptoe, looking out the window).* And right down there's the old grassy knoll, huh.

LOU. Uh-huh.

DUB. How come it's always got to be a Marine, Lou? Every time some lunatic climbs up someplace with his lunch box, his rifle and seventeen sticks of deodorant, it always turns out it's a Marine.

LOU. They're the good shots, I guess.

DUB. So where was you?

LOU. Where was I?

DUB. When it happened. When you heard about it.

LOU. Hell I don't know.

DUB. Thought everybody knew that.

LOU. Not me. Asleep maybe.

DUB. Me, I'm seventeen years old at the lumberyard. Foreman come out. What's his name? Big fat sum bitch. Red-haired, you know. All florid in the face.

LOU. Uh-huh.

DUB. He was glad about it.

LOU. No.

DUB. Yes he was. He was glad about it. Had a big smile on his face.

LOU. Jesus.

DUB. Come out of his office all excited. Big fatso. Had silver glasses, like a beautician. We was on the truck, me and Billy.

LOU. Ended up in Detroit, didn't he?

DUB. Billy?

LOU. Yeah.

DUB. St. Louis.

LOU. That's right.

DUB. Had him that big old baseball mitt, like a lobster claw, remember?

LOU. Yeah. Come runnin' in on the bunt all the time. I got it! I got it!

DUB (*chuckling*). Thought he owned first base.

LOU. Thought he was goin' places.

DUB. He's dead, you know.

LOU. No.

DUB. Died of a glandular, yep.

LOU. I didn't know.

DUB. Well you're down here now, Lou.

LOU. Yeah.

DUB. So where were you?

LOU. Well, lemme see. It was a Friday, wasn't it, he got shot?

DUB. 'Round the lunch hour, yeah.

LOU. Friday noon? Must of been at my momma's, it was a Friday.

DUB. I went in the Marines that Sunday.

LOU. Uh-oh.

DUB. I'm at Belle's house before the plane down to basic, when old Jack Ruby shoots Oswald right on TV.

LOU. Jesus Mary.

DUB. Saw the whole thing, yeah. Next day Monday's the big funeral with the horses and wagons, I'm sittin' at attention some classroom all day long, sergeants takin' turns comin' in screamin' at us.

LOU. Hah.

DUB. Truth is, they didn't know what the hell to do with us that day.

LOU. Stuff like that's how come I joined the Air Force.

DUB. And right here's the very window where he took his shot, huh?

LOU. This is where they say he took it.

DUB. What, you don't believe it?

LOU. I live here, Dub. You live down here you hear things.

DUB. Like what?

LOU. Rather not say.

DUB. Come on.

LOU. No, no. Out of respect to him this museum's for I don't want to say, but there are things said that... Well you just wouldn't believe it if I told you.

DUB. Christ, Lou.

LOU. Dallas it's a funny place, I'm tellin you, Dub. There is people here so rich they can have you shot just for stepping on their grass and can't nobody do a thing about it.

DUB. No.

LOU. When Patty had her gallbladder, she was in the room with a woman was shot by the governor of the state.

DUB. Come on.

LOU. He shot her, Dub. In the abdomen. 'Cause of she was gonna have his child and he didn't want that on account of his wife and his career. Good-lookin' woman too, walkin' to the toilet with that gown wide open right up her back.

DUB. Which governor is that?

LOU. What?

DUB. That shot her.

LOU. I don't know. I don't vote for these people. I don't want nothin' to do with the whole system anymore. All these congress and senators and their blue-ribbon bull-shit. They don't have a clue about it, Dub, about what really happened here in '63. Mafia this and that. Castro. FBI. CIA. It's all nonsense. Just tourist crap for tour-ists.

DUB. Had no idea, I guess.

LOU. Well why would you, living up home? You got to be down here in this place to where you can get the real deal of it, of what really happened, and why. The whole reason for it. Hell, this whole place up here, this mu-seum, this is for children, Dub. Don't even know why I come up here 'cept Patty thought maybe you and Belle'd like it.

DUB. You mean to tell me this Oswald fella he didn't sit right there amongst them boxes there and eat his lunch and fire them shots out the window like they say?

LOU. Ah God, Dub. I just want to have a nice day here with you and Belle.

DUB. Well, I want to have a nice day too, Lou, but it seems to me you the one brought it up.

LOU. I'm just sick of the whole damn mess. Poor old Dallas ain't had a moment's peace behind all this.

DUB. Okay, then. I don't want to—

LOU. All right, all right. Here it is. *(Confidential.)* It's the women, Dub.

DUB. The what?

LOU. The women, the women, goddamnit!

DUB. You mean it was a woman that—

LOU. Shh! Watch your voice now.

DUB. You're saying it was a woman killed Kennedy?

LOU. Not just a woman, Dub.

DUB. Who? You don't mean Jackie.

LOU. I ain't going to lie about it, Dub.

DUB. You're not sayin' old Jackie did it.

LOU. I'm not saying another word.

DUB. Oh, I don't believe that, Lou.

LOU. Don't make it any the less a fact.

DUB. Jesus, she's—she was such a sweet person. So pretty. And her French and stuff.

LOU. Don't you believe it, Dub. They've had it with men, these women. And she's become a underground belief to them, like a, like a, a, a credo.

DUB. But you're a man.

LOU. Yeah.

DUB. So how you know about this, bein' you're a man?

LOU. Patty, she got books.

DUB. Oh.

LOU. All these books around. Must think I can't read, I guess.

DUB. Well I remember old Hillary throwin' a lamp at Clinton once, but—

LOU. Oh Patty'd like to see that Clinton sum bitch castrated.

DUB. Wow, she really got it goin', huh.

LOU. What?

DUB. That she'd nut a man for steppin' out?

LOU. Well that's how they do in orthodox places, isn't it?

DUB. Hey I don't need no Muslim cocksuckers throwin' stones at me. I'm faithful of my own free will.

LOU. You'd like to think so maybe.

DUB. What?

LOU. Your Belle don't strike me as the retiring type, all I'm sayin'.

DUB. She got her opinions, yeah.

LOU. Yeah.

DUB. So what's that supposed to mean?

LOU. Take it easy, Dub. Take it easy.

DUB. Well.

LOU. All I mean to say is gals got more goin' on than what you or I think anymore. And just because we don't understand it don't mean it ain't affectin' our minds and behavior day to day.

DUB. Jeez, Lou.

LOU. I'm scared, Dub. Scared of women. And I'm man enough to say so. The scales are tippin' and they got plans.

DUB. Boy oh boy.

LOU. And it all begun with Jackie Bouvier sending that pathetic Oswald up here to snipe old JFK.

DUB. That's just plain pussywhipped is what that is, Lou.

LOU. And just imagine a whole nation of that, Dub.

DUB. I guess I wouldn't like to.

LOU. Uh-oh. Here comes the wives.

DUB. Whoops.

(DUB and LOU examine the exhibit. BELLE and PATTY enter. The four of them stand looking at the exhibit for a moment, then DUB puts his headphones on and drifts away with LOU. BELLE takes off headphones.)

BELLE *(shaking her head)*. Crazy fool. And in a library, too.

PATTY. Depository.

BELLE. Huh?

PATTY. Was a book depository, what they called it. For books.

BELLE. Shame anyway.

PATTY. Cryin' shame.

BELLE. Such a good-lookin' man too.

PATTY. If you like the type.

BELLE. You mean the aristocrat type.

PATTY. I mean the philanderin' type.

BELLE. Well, they all gone now anyway. Right along with Martin Luther.

PATTY. King?

BELLE. I really cried with that one.

PATTY. Another one with a poor zipper control.

BELLE. Oh that's just the way with leadership, Patty. It's like the bulls do back home.

PATTY. Only the bulls got more class.

BELLE. You don't mean our favorite President?

PATTY. I call him the Pepsodent, on account of his smile.

BELLE. He got a nice smile I think.

PATTY. It's insincere, Belle.

BELLE. Yeah well. Sincerity ain't everything.

PATTY. I first come to Dallas I was such a sucker for that smile, oil-man's smile. Dime a goddamn dozen.

BELLE. Well, you're more sophisticated now.

PATTY. Yeah. Oh Belle, looka here.

BELLE. What?

PATTY (*pointing out window*). See that convertible goin' by down there.

BELLE. Yeah.

PATTY. See there? See that? Snappin' their heads back?

BELLE. What in the heck?

PATTY. That's what kids down here do for fun.

BELLE. That's sick.

PATTY. That's Dallas.

BELLE. Well, I think that's a sick thing.

PATTY. They even got a dance they do called the Kennedy. (*Demonstrates.*)

BELLE. Stop.

PATTY. Strange town, yeah. You wouldn't believe the way they do things sexually.

BELLE. Oh?

PATTY. Yeah, my boss been droppin' the handkerchief for me at work.

BELLE. What's that?

PATTY. It's complicated, what it is.

BELLE. Well tell him to just buzz off, for heaven's sake.

PATTY. She's a woman, Belle.

BELLE. Oh. Well, we get through these things best we can, Patty.

PATTY. Poor old JFK sure didn't.

BELLE. How do you mean?

PATTY. They was lovers, them two.

BELLE. Who two?

PATTY. Him and Oswald. You didn't know that?

BELLE. Oh, come on.

PATTY. Yeah too.

BELLE. They didn't even know each other, Patty.

PATTY. That's what they want you to think.

BELLE. But Oswald he was poor, and married to a Russian wife.

PATTY. That wasn't his wife.

BELLE. No?

PATTY. No way, José. She wasn't even a woman.

BELLE. But they had a daughter, her and Oswald.

PATTY. Wrong.

BELLE. They's pictures of her, Patty. *(PATTY laughs. BELLE points.)* Right over there.

PATTY. You are so naive, girl.

BELLE. Who the heck was Oswald's wife, then?

PATTY. Shhh.

BELLE. Well who was she?

PATTY. She was a he, I'm tellin' you. And he was lovers with JFK back in one of those dormitories up to Harvard that is all give over to this fancy kind of acting out they do.

BELLE. What?

PATTY. Gets worse, too. Boy's father finds out about him and JFK, and sends his kid down here to the oil to get him over his sissy behaviors. But it don't take, and he gets all more and more, 'til he's actually living with Oswald as a woman. And then Kennedy comes down here, and they start making it as a threesome together, which is what they call the Ivy League.

BELLE. Oh my God.

PATTY. Heard it from this woman was shot by the governor.

BELLE. What? Who?

PATTY. Uh-uh. Won't say her name. Me and her was in the hospital together, and she opened my eyes wide, I can tell you. Ain't nothin' been the same since her.

BELLE. How you mean, Patty?

PATTY. I mean she opened my eyes to where I can see, Belle. I can see it all. May not be so pretty as it was, honey, but it is very, very interesting.

BELLE. So why'd Oswald shoot him then?

PATTY. Who?

BELLE. Kennedy. I mean if they was in their Ivy League together.

PATTY. Jealous, I guess.

BELLE. Oh.

PATTY. Just like Lou.

BELLE. And that governor too, huh?

PATTY. That's right. They's all jealous bastards.

BELLE. Dub too, Patty. And I ain't never even give him cause. Not once. But just let me look at another man, and it's Katy bar the door.

PATTY. I know. I know. And they got all these goddamn guns, these guys.

BELLE. Guns all over the place.

PATTY. Which is why I got me one.

BELLE. No!

PATTY. .38 Special, yeah. Been taking lessons on it at the range.

BELLE. Patty!

PATTY. Want to come with me once and shoot?

BELLE. Oh, I couldn't.

PATTY. Lots of women at the range.

BELLE. Really?

PATTY. Bet you'd be a hell of a shot.

BELLE. I got a pretty good eyesight.

PATTY. Well there you go already. Uh-oh. Here they come.

(DUB and LOU re-enter.)

LOU. Well how 'bout it, you gals seen enough?

BELLE. It's sure lots of things to look at, Lou.

PATTY. She still ain't seen that Zapruder mess over there.

BELLE. Well.

LOU. Plus we got the Conspiracy Museum.

DUB. Oh I don't know, Lou.

LOU. Give you the whole other point of view, Dub.

DUB. Maybe tomorrow, yeah.

LOU. It's a hoot.

PATTY. They don't want to go to the Conspiracy, Lou.

LOU. Okay. Okay. What say we go and get some Mexican?

BELLE. There you go.

LOU. They got fantastic Mexican down here.

DUB. Great.

PATTY. You want to there's a gift shop, while me and
    Lou we get the car.

LOU. Yeah, they got all kinds of stuff. Mugs and stuff.
    Show you where you been to.

PATTY. Something for your grandkids, yeah.

BELLE. That's a nice idea.

LOU. We'll meet you 'round the back.

(LOU and PATTY exit.)

BELLE. You want to see that Zapruder thingy?

DUB. You can look at it if you want.

BELLE. That old Patty she's—she's different, Dub. You get along with Lou okay?

DUB. I don't know, Belle, all this Kennedy, Kennedy, Kennedy, Kennedy.

BELLE. Yeah.

DUB. It's just—heck he's just a man, wasn't he? Come out between of a woman's legs same as you and me and all the rest?

BELLE. That's right.

DUB. Wasn't no saint we got to worship and adore and get all worked up about.

BELLE. I guess not, but—

DUB. Well, I don't want to buy no dead man's mug.

BELLE. Okay, Dub.

DUB. I don't want it, Belle. I just don't want that for my grandkids.

BELLE. Dub, what's—

DUB. I DON'T WANT IT I SAID!

BELLE. Then we don't get it, honey. Okay? Dub? Okay?

DUB. You you like me, don't you, Belle?

BELLE. Why sure I like you, Dub.

DUB. And and you'll—you'll be kind to me, won't you?

BELLE. What do you mean, Dub? You know I'll be kind to you. You know that.

DUB. Okay, because—okay.

BELLE. You okay, then?

DUB. Let's just go, okay?

BELLE. Okay. Okay. We'll go. Let's just go.

DUB (*staring at exhibit*). Okay. Okay. Okay then.

END OF PLAY

LAYLA MISERABLES

By

Olga Humphrey

Layla Misérables premiered at the New Georges' "Performathon 2000," NYC, and was produced by Pandora's Box Theater, Buffalo, N.Y., in 2001.

CHARACTERS

NORMAN: A down-on-his-luck persimmon farmer.
MATHILDE: Norman's wife.*
JENNIFER ANNE: Norman and Mathilde's 10-year-old daughter.*
SALES CLERK*
CHAVERT: A police constable.*

* All of the women characters are played by one actor.

SETTING: Paris. The play contains a number of short scenes requiring flexible staging.

TIME: No rhyme or reason.

LAYLA MISERABLES

AT THE CURTAIN: *Enter NORMAN, dressed in 19th-century garb. His countenance is woeful, his shoulders slumped. Every day is a bad one. He turns to the audience, his only friend.*

NORMAN. If the truth is to be told, mine is a tragic tale, one of unbearable sadness. Little did I realize that when my beloved Mathilde decided to leave me, I would begin my dark odyssey.

(Enter MATHILDE in the equivalent of a 19th-century housecoat.)

MATHILDE. Although my heart is fuller than the moon, I must leave you, Norman.

NORMAN. But why, my love?

MATHILDE *(dreamy-eyed)*. To finally achieve my girlhood dream.

NORMAN. And what is that?

MATHILDE. To become a broken-down, pox-infested, toothless whore on the streets of Paris.

NORMAN. But, Mathilde, we have built a life together as persimmon farmers.

MATHILDE. There's not much variation in that, Norman. But think of the infinite variety inherent in skanky street life, my dear. Oh, Norman, it will be so glorious. I can't wait to pick my first louse tick out of my matted hair.

NORMAN. I don't know what to say, Mathilde.

MATHILDE. That's your problem, Norman. You never know what to say or do. I want to ride the wild pony.

NORMAN. Isn't that dangerous?

MATHILDE. I'm gonna live and live now, Norman! Oh, how I got what it takes. I know how. Hey, Mr. Johnstein, here I am!

NORMAN. Is he your first client?

(MATHILDE turns to go. NORMAN realizes something.)

NORMAN. Wait! Mathilde, what of our four little ones? Wee Jennifer Anne, budding Mary Lou, snot-nosed Edgar, and stalwart Keanu?

MATHILDE. Fuck 'em.

NORMAN. Mathilde, please don't abandon me and our life together. Our babes, our home, the persimmon fields we've plowed.

MATHILDE. They grow on trees, you numbskull. No wonder you've always been such a shitty persimmon farmer.

NORMAN. Well, what of the grog by the fireplace, the warmth of the hearth, a simple hearty repast, the conjugal bed?

(MATILDA lets out a huge yawn. She turns, walks off. A DOOR SLAMS.)

NORMAN. I suppose that door slamming means she's left me. Mathilde? Mathilde? Oh, woe.

(LIGHTS change. NORMAN is sweeping. His daughter JENNIFER ANNE, 10, enters. She is played by the same actress, on her knees.)

JENNIFER ANNE. Papa?

NORMAN. Yes, Wee Jennifer Anne?

JENNIFER ANNE. We're hungry.

NORMAN. I know, my little one. Come sit on Papa's lap. *(He bravely tries to hoist her up.)* My, you've become heavy.

JENNIFER ANNE. Are you saying I'm fat?

NORMAN. You're growing. You're a fine, growing young girl. Why don't you just lean on Papa's lap instead. *(A beat as he gazes at her lovingly.)* You do look so like your mother.

JENNIFER ANNE. Papa, why did Mama leave?

NORMAN. To ride the wild pony.

JENNIFER ANNE. I want to ride the wild pony, too.

NORMAN. You don't want to do that, my dear. He'll throw you off and crack your skull open and your brains will spill out in a hot, steaming heap.

JENNIFER ANNE. Mama said you were a lousy lay, Papa. What does that mean?

NORMAN. It means I kept rolling over in bed all through the night. I stole the blankets in my sleep. I snored.

JENNIFER ANNE. She left because she couldn't get a good night's sleep?

NORMAN. That's it.

JENNIFER ANNE. Is that why that man came in the afternoon?

NORMAN. What man?

JENNIFER ANNE. Mr. Johnstein. They always went into the bedroom. He was a good lay. Mama looked very bright-eyed and bushy-tailed when they came out.

NORMAN. Yes, well. Why don't I go and see if the persimmon fields are ready to be harvested, my little one.

JENNIFER ANNE. That's why we're hungry, Papa. You're an incompetent boob. There are no persimmons growing in the fields. They grow on trees. What's wrong with you? Can't you get your act together for once?

NORMAN. Jennifer Anne!

JENNIFER ANNE. I'm sorry, Papa. It's just with Mama gone, I believe I and the other little ones are in deep shit.

NORMAN *(starts to cry)*. I'm a man. What do you expect?

JENNIFER ANNE. I know, Papa. I know. I love you. I will try to help you, as useless as you are because of your dingle.

NORMAN. As my eldest daughter, I must ask of you something that no man should have to ask of his little ones.

JENNIFER ANNE. Yes, Papa.

NORMAN. Now that your beloved Mama...

JENNIFER ANNE. I wouldn't go that far.

NORMAN. Now that your dear...

JENNIFER ANNE. Uh-uh.

NORMAN. Now that your well-liked...

JENNIFER ANNE. Nope.

NORMAN. Now that your tolerable...

JENNIFER ANNE. Sold.

NORMAN. ...Mama has left us, may I ask that you become mama to your siblings?

JENNIFER ANNE. That's a drag, Papa.

NORMAN. I know I am asking you to give up some of your childhood years. For you see, the persimmons are dying, my dear. A horrible frost as chilly as your Mama's heart is settling in over the land.

JENNIFER ANNE. What are we going to eat? All we have in the fridge is that nasty filet mignon we give the dog.

NORMAN. I vow as I stand here today: My babies will not eat dog food!!!

JENNIFER ANNE. You go, Papa!

NORMAN. Run along, now, and scrape the scum off something, my dear. I'm going to buy us some bread.

JENNIFER ANNE. Fat chance.

NORMAN. What did you just say?

JENNIFER ANNE. Rye pumpernickel.

NORMAN. Oh. If they have it, I will certainly return with a nice big rye pumpernickel loaf. Now waddle off, my dear, waddle off.

(JENNIFER ANNE exits, giving her father a dirty look before she goes.

LIGHTS change. NORMAN stands alone. He addresses the AUDIENCE.)

NORMAN. With the coins in my pocket, I set off for the baker's, but on the way, I stopped at... Dare I tell you? *(A beat. Anguish.)* I stopped at... *(Tortured.)* That place. *(A beat.)* My curiosity got the better of my empty stomach.

(A SALES CLERK enters. A small wrapped box sits on a stand.)

NORMAN. I noticed you have a sale.

SALES CLERK. This is tax-free week. And to further entice, we've slashed our prices by fifty percent.

NORMAN. Do you take coins?

SALES CLERK. We prefer plastic, but I can make an exception this once.

NORMAN. Thank you.

SALES CLERK. First time here?

NORMAN. Yes, I was on my way to buy bread.

SALES CLERK. That's what they all say.

NORMAN. I'm down on my luck. My wife's left me. I have four hungry mouths to feed. I'm a failure as a persimmon farmer. The women in my life scorn me.

SALES CLERK. You want the "Layla" then.

NORMAN. The "Layla"?

(NORMAN looks at the gift-wrapped box. NOTE: Exactly what the "Layla" is should be vague, but the package should be small enough to hold in one's hand.)

SALES CLERK. She asks no questions. She thinks you're grand. She looks up to you. She loves you to death, you failure, you.

NORMAN. I...

SALES CLERK. She senses your loneliness. She's a pal. She's blonde, if you prefer.

NORMAN. Blonde? Really?

SALES CLERK. Many feel that blonde is neater, tidier, more ordered, less threatening perhaps.

NORMAN. Blonde for me. Does she speak?

SALES CLERK. Her lips are mum.

NORMAN. Oh. Can I teach her to speak at some point? Just to say nice things, like "I love you," "You're swell," "My those are some big persimmons you've got there."

SALES CLERK. I'm sure that can be managed.

NORMAN. I would like to take the Layla.

SALES CLERK. Three coins, sir.

NORMAN. Oh, I'm afraid I have less than I thought. One coin?

SALES CLERK. Three coins, sir.

NORMAN. But...

SALES CLERK. Three coins, sir...

NORMAN. Can I give you this as a deposit?

SALES CLERK. Layla will lay, but she won't layaway. I'm sorry, sir.

NORMAN. Is there a cheaper model?

SALES CLERK. There is the Babette. But even we don't know where she's been, sir. Of course, there are those rumors about Des Moines.

NORMAN. Well, thank you for your time.

(SALES CLERK turns away and exits.)

NORMAN *(to AUDIENCE)*. I had to have her. She was my only hope of happiness. I did what every red-blooded, pathetic persimmon farmer would do in my situation. I pilfered her. *(He grabs the Layla box and runs.)*

(LIGHTS change. NORMAN stationary running.)

NORMAN. I ran and I ran and I ran. And I ran and I ran and I ran. And I ran and I ran and I ran, until ... I took a break.

(Enter CONSTABLE CHAVERT.)

CHAVERT *(to AUDIENCE)*. I saw him as he ran from the store. A look of fear intermingled with hope. A common thief. In his hands, the Layla. It was then that I knew that I would run to the ends of the earth to catch him. You see, that was the last model that existed. The last one in this entire world. I was on my way to buy it. I had bought all the rest and destroyed them. Why? Because in a past life, I was Layla. But now I am Constable Chavert.

NORMAN. Guzundheit!

CHAVERT. Not that old joke again! You'd better run fast, little man.

(NORMAN is stationary running. CHAVERT is stationary running behind him. NORMAN is faster, leaving CHAVERT in his dust.)

NORMAN. And I ran and I ran and I ran. Someone was behind me. Someone with a look of fierce determination. Someone who would never let me have a moment's peace.

(LIGHTS change. NORMAN's home.)

NORMAN. I arrived home.
JENNIFER ANNE *(from offstage)*. Bread, Papa?

(NORMAN exits. A DOOR SLAMS. JENNIFER ANNE enters.)

JENNIFER ANNE. Where's the bread, Papa? *(STRANGE NOISES and WEIRD MUSIC emanate from offstage.)* Papa? Papa? What's going on in there, Papa?

(The STRANGE NOISES and WEIRD MUSIC continue. JENNIFER ANNE listens in rapt attention. NORMAN enters. He has a backpack on.)

NORMAN. Jennifer Anne, I must leave you.
JENNIFER ANNE. Why?
NORMAN. Because I am a thief. A constable will be here to arrest me shortly. But have no fear. I am now a happy man.
JENNIFER ANNE. Does it have to do with all that psychedelic music coming from the bedroom?
NORMAN. You're wise beyond your years, child.
JENNIFER ANNE. Run, Papa, run. *(She exits.)*
NORMAN *(to AUDIENCE)*. And so I ran...

(LIGHTS change. NORMAN stationary running.)

NORMAN. And I ran and I ran and I ran...

(CHAVERT enters stationary running.)

CHAVERT. And I ran after him.

NORMAN & CHAVERT. And we ran and we ran and we ran, until we collided.

NORMAN. After all, this is a ten-minute play and we're already running long.

CHAVERT. You will go to jail, sir. Ay, you will fester in a dank cell now that I've caught you.

NORMAN. You are?

CHAVERT. Chavert!

NORMAN. Guzundheit!

CHAVERT. With hard labor added for telling old jokes.

NORMAN. May I ask what the charges are?

CHAVERT. You have stolen the Layla.

NORMAN. I had no choice. It was out of love, madam, because I was out of love. I will serve my time, but let her stay with me.

CHAVERT. She will be entered into evidence and then destroyed, sir!

NORMAN. But why?

CHAVERT. Because she is me.

NORMAN. You are the Layla?

CHAVERT. I am, sir.

NORMAN. You're quite good.

CHAVERT. It's what *you* bring to the Layla that counts, fool.

NORMAN. Then why destroy her?

CHAVERT. A past life that is always one step behind me. But now I can finally be free of it.

NORMAN. What else did you do in this past life?

CHAVERT. It was sordid.

NORMAN. Your heart is pendulous.

CHAVERT. Say what?

NORMAN. Heavy. I sense these things in a woman.

CHAVERT. Not many men do.

NORMAN. I would like to know. To listen.

CHAVERT. You would?

NORMAN. Unburden yourself. Have no fear.

CHAVERT. I was a hootchie dancer. I told bad jokes. I introduced myself as *(sneezing)* "Chavert."

NORMAN. I understand now.

CHAVERT. I wore marshmallows on the tips of my breasts. My act was so hot that by the end of it, they were toasted.

NORMAN. Oh!

CHAVERT. And to think I always wanted to devote myself to the good of man.

NORMAN. But that's exactly what you were doing.

CHAVERT. It didn't end there. I shot persimmons out of my womanhood as the "Marseillaise" played in the background. At least I was proud of my country.

NORMAN. Did you say persimmons?

CHAVERT. Yes, why?

NORMAN. I am a persimmon farmer.

CHAVERT. So misunderstood.

NORMAN. The ripening...

CHAVERT. Yes.

NORMAN. ...process.

CHAVERT. Yes.

NORMAN. They have to over-ripen, in effect.

CHAVERT. Yes.

NORMAN. Practically rot.

CHAVERT. I'm embarrassed to admit...

NORMAN. What?

CHAVERT. I always used to believe they grew from the ground.

NORMAN. On my land that's where they come from... I think.

CHAVERT. But how...

NORMAN. It happens. Sometimes in life, things simply happen.

CHAVERT. Sir.

NORMAN. Norman.

CHAVERT. Perhaps we can forget this indiscretion.

NORMAN. Thank you. *(Giving her the Layla.)* I guess I should return this to you.

CHAVERT. Yes.

NORMAN. Constable?

CHAVERT. Yes?

NORMAN. Perhaps you would enjoy paying a visit someday. During the harvest, I could pick a few...

CHAVERT. And I could shoot a few... *(Beat.)* That would be lovely, sir.

NORMAN. Good day, Constable.

CHAVERT. Good day, Norman.

(She walks off. NORMAN looks after her for a second, then turns to the AUDIENCE.)

NORMAN. And so, a tale of woe now becomes a tale of hope. Pathetic persimmon farmers out there... *(Peers out, perhaps indicates someone.)* I see you. Do not turn away in shame. Sit straight. Sit proud. And plant that seed of love.

END OF PLAY

THE COMPETENT HEART

By
Pat Montley

The Competent Heart was a final-finalist in the 1996 Actors Theatre of Louisville National Ten-Minute Play Contest, and was featured in the Love Creek Short Play Festival at the Harold Clurman Theatre, New York City, 1996. It was also produced by The Women's Project at Theatre Project, Baltimore, 1996.

CHARACTERS

TERRY: The proprietor, either sex; any age; a very competent pragmatist.

CHRIS: The customer, either sex; any age; a less-than-competent romantic.

SETTING: An intimate bookstore.
TIME: The present.

THE COMPETENT HEART

AT THE CURTAIN: *TERRY is shelving books. CHRIS approaches, browses through the books in one book-case.*

TERRY. May I help you?

CHRIS. I want to be a competent person.

TERRY. Excuse me?

CHRIS. My significant other is tired of being the competent one.

TERRY. Your significant other?

CHRIS. My ... domestic partner.

TERRY. I see.

CHRIS. Do you?

TERRY. So you thought ... *(Referring to case where CHRIS has been browsing.)* you'd try poetry.

CHRIS. I always go to the poetry section first. That's how I tell if it's a good bookstore.

TERRY. And ... is it?

CHRIS. You have the Singleton translation of Dante.

TERRY. Yes.

CHRIS. The Sayers is better.

TERRY. The Singleton is more faithful to the original.

CHRIS. But it isn't even in verse. Anybody can translate. It takes another poet to translate into *terza rima.*

TERRY. Some people don't want to read "another poet." They want to read Dante.

CHRIS *(with disdain).* In prose?

TERRY *(conceding).* The Sayers is out of print.

CHRIS. Ah. *(Beat.)*

TERRY. What kind of competence are you looking for?

CHRIS. I'm not sure. Remember it isn't my idea.

TERRY *(inviting).* Speculate.

CHRIS. Well...perhaps omniscience... *(Beat.)* though I don't think omnipotence is expected.

TERRY. That must be a relief.

CHRIS. Yes...something short of that.

TERRY. How short?

CHRIS. Somewhere between helpless and all-powerful.

TERRY. Do you want to be...capable, adequate, satisfactory?

CHRIS. At least.

TERRY. Efficient, productive, on top of things?

CHRIS. Probably.

TERRY. Authoritative, imperative, controlling—

CHRIS. Definitely not.

TERRY. Good. Now we've settled on degree. How about field of activity?

CHRIS. That's a hard one. I think the disappointment is pretty...universal.

TERRY. Whose?

CHRIS. My significant other's.

TERRY. Are you sure?

CHRIS. It felt that way to me.

TERRY. I'm sorry. *(Pause.)* So you'd like to...

CHRIS. Become a competent person.

TERRY. Yes. Were any specifics mentioned?

CHRIS. Medicine.

TERRY. Medicine?

CHRIS. I need to know stuff.

TERRY. Like?

CHRIS. Like what kind of food not to eat if you've been throwing up.

TERRY. Hmm...

CHRIS. And what to do if somebody mistakes the mosquito-bite drops for the eye drops, and puts them in.

TERRY. Ouch.

CHRIS. Oh yes—and the difference between aspirin and Tylenol.

TERRY. The hard questions.

CHRIS. Yeah.

TERRY *(crossing to shelf)*. How about... *(Perusing shelf, locating a book.)* Complete Guide to Symptoms, Illness & Surgery?

CHRIS *(taking the tome, reading cover)*. "796 symptoms, 520 illnesses, 160 surgeries," *(Opening to various pages at random.)* "Alzheimer's...anxiety...hot flashes ...impotence...PMS...genital warts...hemorrhoid removal"...all the important stuff. *(Turning to last part.)* "Aspirin" is not in the index. *(Returns book.)*

TERRY *(pulling another book)*. This one has a good medication guide. *(Hands book to CHRIS.)* It's in the back.

CHRIS *(checking)*. Aspirin's not on this list either.

TERRY. Look under "analgesic" or "antipyretic."

CHRIS *(looking)*. Wow! Here it is. Just like you said. Now how did you know that? I admire a person who knows things like that.

TERRY. Thank you.

CHRIS. Now see, if I had you at home, I wouldn't have to buy this book. *(Pause)*

TERRY. What other?

CHRIS. Other what?

TERRY. Areas of desired competence?

CHRIS (beat). Domestic engineering.

TERRY. Like plumbing?

CHRIS. Yeah, like how to adjust one of those thingama-jigs in the back of the toilet.

TERRY. A ball-cock assembly?

CHRIS. That's the thing.

TERRY (pulls a book from another bookcase). Try the Home Repair Handbook. (Gives it to CHRIS.)

CHRIS. Will this say what to do when the pipes freeze?

TERRY (shrugs). Warm them with a hair dryer.

CHRIS. Look, is there a gene for knowing this stuff or what? I mean where did you learn that?

TERRY. I don't know.

CHRIS. Come on—did you read that in this book?

TERRY. No. But you can.

CHRIS. You probably even know how to install a dimmer switch.

TERRY. They come in handy, don't they?

CHRIS. So—you're a romantic.

TERRY (ignoring this). Anything else?

CHRIS. Did I say something wrong?

TERRY. Is there another competence you want to develop?

CHRIS. Yes. I'd like to be better at...looking after...taking care of...living things.

TERRY. What kind of living things?

CHRIS. Well...plants?

TERRY (reaching to another shelf). You could read The New York Times Book of House Plants. (Hands it to CHRIS.)

CHRIS (paging through). Pictures. That's good. Oh—here's one we have—with the little pink flowers.

TERRY (*just glancing at the page upside down, then looking at CHRIS*). Cyclamen. Yes, beautiful blooms. Requires a lot of care though: just the right temperature, the right amount of light and water, daily misting, the pebble base. You have to really love it.

CHRIS. Oh, I do. I do. But sometimes it's hard to know ... what a living thing needs.

TERRY. Well, the book is pretty specific about—

CHRIS (*interrupting*). Yeah, right. So ... if I read these books ... will that do it?

TERRY. Hmm ... assuming you apply what you learn.

CHRIS. I mean—you seem real clear on it—is that all there is to competence?

TERRY. It's a good start.

CHRIS. Tell me, do you believe in talking to plants?

TERRY. Some people do. Do you?

CHRIS. I read to them. I believe all living things need ... poetry.

TERRY. But could your cyclamen live on poetry?

CHRIS. Could my cyclamen live without poetry? (*Takes a volume of Emily Dickinson from the poetry shelf, opens to a familiar page, and recites without having to read it, looking at TERRY.*)

> "It's all I have to bring today—
> This, and my heart beside—
> This, and my heart, and all the fields—
> And all the meadows wide—
> Be sure you count—should I forget
> Some one the sum could tell—
> This, and my heart, and all the Bees
> Which in the Clover dwell."

(*CHRIS slowly closes book and replaces it on shelf. Beat.*)

TERRY. Chris...

CHRIS (*takes a credit card from pocket, hands it to TERRY*). Put the books on my VISA. (*Starts to leave, turns back.*) I'll make your favorite quiche for dinner.

TERRY. But the oven...

CHRIS. Will be fixed by the time you get home.

TERRY. You can't fix a gas stove!

CHRIS. No, but the repair person I called this morning can.

(*Beat. TERRY kisses the card and tips it toward CHRIS, who smiles in return and exits. LIGHTS.*)

END OF PLAY

TALKING ABOUT IT

By
Nikki Harmon

Talking About It was a finalist in the 1995 Actors Theatre of Louisville National Ten-Minute Play Contest, and was premiered by Pot Luck Productions, Kansas City, Mo., 1997.

CHARACTERS

OPEL
TROPIE: Opel's best friend.

SETTING: An outdoor café in the spring. The other tables are empty.

TIME: The present, late afternoon.

TALKING ABOUT IT

AT THE CURTAIN: *OPEL and TROPIE sit silently, nursing their cups of coffee. OPEL has a scarf covering her head.*

OPEL. I'm dying.
TROPIE. I know.
OPEL. You know?
TROPIE. Yes.
OPEL. That I'm dying?
TROPIE. Yes.
OPEL. Who told you?
TROPIE. Your doctor.
OPEL. My doctor told you that I was dying?
TROPIE. Yes.
OPEL. Oh.

(The WOMEN sit in silence for a while.)

OPEL. It's against the law, isn't it? To tell.
TROPIE. I don't know.
OPEL. I'm sure it is. Doctors. Lawyers. Priests. They're not supposed to tell. They take oaths about that kind of thing. Never to tell. I don't think it's right. I think people need to know about people. Need to know if someone they know is, you know...
TROPIE. Dying.
OPEL. Yes. *(Pause.)* Did you ask? I mean, were you the one who brought up the subject? Phoned up my doctor,

went into his office and said, "So, how's Opel doing, Doc? She going to hang around a little longer or bite the big one?" Or did he pick up his address book and say to himself one day, "I think I'll call Opel's best friend. The only best friend she's got left since she took to wearing that headgear." Channel scarves are supposed to be worn around the neck, draped ever so casually over the shoulders, not around a head where there used to be hair. That sounds better than bald, don't you think? "Where there used to be hair." Yes, I like that much better. So, which was it? Who picked up the phone first? You or him?

TROPIE. Does it matter?

OPEL. Yes, it matters.

TROPIE. I did.

OPEL. Then it's all right. It's not as if he phoned you up one sunny afternoon on his own and you weren't prepared to talk about the guy with the sickle. The big "D" word.

TROPIE. It was raining that day.

OPEL. So much the better. I'd hate to think you were kept in on a lovely day hearing that I was dying. Plans to go to the beach. Had your towel and your Coppertone and a good book folded into your backpack, halfway out the door and he laid it on you. Phoned you up and told you. Picked the exact moment you were putting on your Walkman and slipping in a favorite CD to call and tell you. Did he say it outright or did he beat around the proverbial bush? "Hello, Tropie. Opel is dying." Or did he ask how you were first? Chat about the weather? How Jake and the kids were? Reminisce about this or that. People you both knew. People walking around doing things, planning things, next year's vacations...

TROPIE. Outright. He told me outright. He felt that since you had no family and that he'd known me as long as he knew you...

OPEL. I'm sorry.

TROPIE. It's all right. I prefer things that way. Straightforward. Get it out and over with. No lingering. To the point and have it done with. Straightforward.

OPEL. That's good, then. *(Pause.)* I'm dying.

TROPIE. I know.

OPEL. Of cancer.

TROPIE. Yes. I know.

OPEL. Not AIDS.

TROPIE. No, not AIDS.

OPEL. If I have a transfusion in the end, I mean right at the end, when they're talking about pulling the plug, taking out the tube, turning off the switch, all the things they do at the end, and the blood is tainted and I die, will they say I died of AIDS or cancer? I mean if I have cancer and AIDS gets me first which one gets the credit?

TROPIE. What difference does it make?

OPEL. It makes a difference. Who do people donate to? "Donations appreciated in lieu of flowers to..." You have to tell people where to send their money. You can't have people writing checks to one and it should go to the other. That's not fair. And what statistic do I become? That's important. It could mean the difference between one getting a research grant and not the other. The cutoff could be "one million more deaths" and I get put on the wrong list. What if they both only need one more person to get the money, and the wrong one gets me? Someone else's disease would get the money, not my disease, not the one that gets me in the end. It could be the grant that finds the cure. I'd be the one who decided if cancer or AIDS gets cured first. It's a big decision. I have to get on the right list. Tropie, you'll see to it that I get on the right list?

TROPIE. I'll see to it.

OPEL. Tropie.

TROPIE. Yes.

OPEL. I'm afraid.

TROPIE. I know.

OPEL. Do you think there'll be pain? I don't want there to be any pain. I couldn't stand it if there was pain. I never could stand pain. I was always the one who cried the loudest when I fell down as a child. Pain frightens me. That's the reason I never had children. The pain. I used to watch you with your children and wonder how you got through it. Through childbirth. Did you know that? Did you know that's what I was thinking when I saw you with your kids?

TROPIE. No.

OPEL. You'd be pushing Sally or Timmy on the swing and thinking about what you were going to make for dinner that night, and I'd be thinking about eighteen hours of excruciatingly painful childbirth. Other people saw a mother with her children, and I saw a woman who'd survived pain. I'd think, "No children. No pain." It's not that I didn't want children. I wanted children, but the pain, I couldn't stand the thought of the pain.

TROPIE. There won't be any pain, Opel. I promise.

OPEL. Good. (Pause.) Tropie.

TROPIE. Yes?

OPEL. I don't want to be dependent on anyone. Feeding me. Cutting up my food and feeding me. Staring at me, waiting for me to finish chewing, then shoving in another forkful and sitting back and staring at me again, waiting for me to finish chewing so they could shove in something else. I don't want it to be like that. If I can't feed myself I don't want anyone else doing it for me. And I don't want people carrying me to the toilet. I couldn't stand that. People there with me while I was on the toilet. Standing there with me while I was...I'd hate that... Tropie?

TROPIE. Yes?

OPEL. You won't let that happen to me, will you?

TROPIE. No.

OPEL. People carrying me back and forth. Picking me up and putting me in a bathtub like a baby. Washing me all over. Scrubbing me down. Rubbing a washcloth all over me. Over parts of me *I* don't even look at. Wiping me at the toilet. You'll stop them, won't you? You won't let them do that to me, will you? To humiliate me like that. Please promise you won't let them do that to me. *(TROPIE doesn't answer.)* Tropie? You won't, will you?

TROPIE. No.

OPEL. And the pain? You won't let there be pain? I couldn't take the pain.

TROPIE. No pain.

OPEL. Good.

(The WOMEN sit in silence.)

OPEL. The roses need pruning every year. They need to be cared for. I couldn't stand it if they died, too.

TROPIE. Jake will do it. He's very good with flowers.

OPEL. I want him to start tomorrow.

TROPIE. There's no rush.

OPEL. Have him look at the roses tomorrow.

TROPIE. If you want, but maybe we should wait. The doctor said there's always a chance of remission.

OPEL. Tomorrow.

TROPIE. Tomorrow.

OPEL. Thank you.

(The WOMEN sit in silence.)

OPEL. Tropie.

TROPIE. Yes.

OPEL. How will you...?

TROPIE. Shhhhhh.

OPEL. I want to know.

TROPIE. I don't know yet.

OPEL. When the time comes...

TROPIE. I'll know.

OPEL. I don't think I could do it for you.

TROPIE. I know.

OPEL. It doesn't mean I care less for you, that you're not my best friend. It just means...

TROPIE. You don't have to say it.

OPEL. That we're different. Opposite. The more opposite the friend the better the friendship. That's a saying, isn't it? I think it is. If it's not it should be. It's true with us. We do different things. You cook, I build shelves. I sew, you cut patterns backwards. *(Pause.)* It doesn't mean I wouldn't want to. If you asked I'd want to.

TROPIE. I wouldn't ask.

OPEL. Because you know me. You know what I can't do. We're that close. We think each other's thoughts. Know what the other can and can't do. Not doesn't want to, but can't. That's right, isn't it?

TROPIE. That's right.

OPEL. You know I'd want to.

TROPIE. I know.

OPEL. Jake *will* come tomorrow?

TROPIE. Yes. Tomorrow.

(The WOMEN sit in silence.)

OPEL. Tropie.

TROPIE. Yes.

OPEL. I love you.

TROPIE. I know.

(The WOMEN sit in silence, sipping their coffee, as the LIGHTS fade out.)

END OF PLAY

REVELATION 24:12

By

Linda Eisenstein

Revelation 24:12 was first produced by Love Creek Productions, 1998 at the Harold Clurman Theatre in New York City. It featured Annette Sydow and Jim Coffey and was directed by Michael Cuevas.

The play was a finalist in the 1999 Religion & Theatre One-Act Competition, sponsored by the Association for Theatre in Higher Education.

It also was a winner of the 2000 Get to the Point! One-Act Competition and was produced in "Summer Shorts: A Festival of 10-Minute Plays," University of Wisconsin at Stevens Point, 2000. The production featured Betsy Skowbo and Micah Rademacher and was directed by Ellen Margolis.

Revelation 24:12 was previously published in the journal *FemSpec*, Volume 1, issue 2, 2000.

CHARACTERS

JANNA and DOUG: A married couple.

SETTING: The bedroom of Janna and Doug.
TIME: The present. Night.

REVELATION 24:12

AT THE CURTAIN: *Early a.m., before it's fully light. JANNA and DOUG in bed. JANNA is sitting bolt upright, as though in a trance, her eyes staring wide open; DOUG is asleep.*

SFX: Some kind of weird synthy sound—a cross between music-buzzing-humming.

JANNA. Oh yes. The way it shimmers, and—yes oh please— *(She holds out her hand—she gasps. SFX: Sound cuts out suddenly.)* Something. Something's in here. Doug. Douglas! *(DOUG starts.)* Incredible. It's— Oh my God. Doug. There was something in the room. Looming over the bed.

DOUG. Not one of those dreams again.

JANNA. No. Different. Doug, wake up. This is important. Eyes. And wings.

DOUG. Honey, you had a bad dream.

JANNA. Not bad. More like—awesome. *(Sniffing the air.)* Oh my God. It wasn't a dream. Can you smell that? It was here. It shimmered, and spoke, and it left...its spoor. Can't you smell that??

DOUG. What.

JANNA. It smells like... *(Sniffs.)* ...pot roast. With onion gravy. It smells like Gramma's pot roast. It's a sign, Doug, it's a sign. It wanted me to have proof.

DOUG. Proof of what? That you miss your grandmother's pot roast? *(Groans, turns over.)* Just give me ten more minutes.

JANNA. It wanted to show me something familiar. It was so unbelievably strange, so alien—but it didn't want me to be afraid. Come over here. Smell that.

DOUG *(sniffing)*. I'll be damned. It does smell like your Gram's.

JANNA. It was real. Not a dream. More like a revelation.

DOUG. Maybe it means you need to change your diet. It's winter, maybe you need more protein.

JANNA. I have to write this down, try to remember every moment. It's important. *(Sniffs again.)* God, I miss her gravy. I'd kill for the recipe.

DOUG. Janna, okay, it's weird, but let's not turn it into a big deal. Let's be logical. So you've been missing your grandmother, and you dream about her—

JANNA. I didn't dream about Gramma.

DOUG. And your longing somehow transformed itself into an olfactory hallucination. Which somehow I can smell, but I liked her pot roast too, so it's not that weird.

JANNA. What I saw was *nothing* like Gram. Unless Gram went to heaven and came back as a nine-foot being with six wings and about four hundred eyes. *(Pause.)*

DOUG *(suddenly very awake)*. What? What did you say?

JANNA. Eyes. More eyes that I could...

DOUG *(becoming excited)*. Holy cow. That sounds like a seraph.

JANNA. A what?

DOUG. A seraph. Plural, seraphim. As in, "Seraphim and cherubim bow down before Thee." Angels. The big guys.

JANNA. You think I saw an angel?

DOUG. The ones they always put on the greeting cards are the cute little cherub ones. But there are others.

JANNA. God, it could have been an angel. The way it shimmered—it could have been. Where's my journal?

DOUG. Now, the seraphim—hoo mama. You wouldn't want to meet the seraphim in a dark alley. Multiple wings, more than one face. Revelations 24:12, I think. Or is it 12:24? Where's a Bible when you need one?

JANNA. It had such a glow around it. Blue and white with pink fiery twinkly streaks and sparks.

DOUG. Blue's a good sign. Benign. Incarnations of the Blessed Virgin usually come in blue, you know.

JANNA. Not really a blue-blue—more like a rainbow that reminded me of blue.

DOUG. An aura.

JANNA *(becoming preoccupied with her dream journal)*. Yes.

DOUG. Shoot! I can't believe I slept through it. These visitations are well-documented phenomena. Especially around the millennia. I mean, go to any occult bookstore. Shelves and shelves of revelations, all kinds of people are writing them down these days. Especially with self-publishing. "What Ilium of Zorcon revealed to me about Real Estate Investment Trusts"—have you surfed the Web lately?

JANNA. Stop talking. I'm trying to remember it all.

DOUG. Did he say anything?

JANNA. It wasn't... What are you doing?

DOUG *(he's found the Bible, is looking through it)*. Checking the references. There are a lot of angelic visitations in here. Maybe we can find out who it was.

JANNA. Why does it have to sound like something that's already written down? Isn't that the point of a revelation?: something new. And anyway, the revelation came to me, not you.

DOUG. How do you know it was aimed at you? I was in the room. I know more about spiritual phenomenon than you do. I was the one who thought about going to seminary. I had even applied.

JANNA. You were fast asleep!

DOUG. Like the disciples. Jesus kept having to wake them up.

JANNA. The revelation was to me. I can't believe you're trying to take credit for my revelation! This is typical. You can't *wait* to get your hands on it.

DOUG. Why wouldn't I have one?

JANNA. Like I'm taking a message for you, your secretary? You are unbelievable.

DOUG. All right, all right. And the angel saith unto Janna—I admit it does sound better that way—and the angel saith—well, what did it say? You've got me sucked in now, don't hold back. "And the angel saith unto her:"

JANNA. "Behold."

DOUG. Ah, good. Behold what?

JANNA. Just, "behold." Then she—he—it just stood there.

DOUG. Not much of a message. There's usually more. "And the angel said unto them, 'Behold.' And they were sore afraid." What are you supposed to behold?

JANNA. I don't really know. It's not as though it was pointing at anything in the general vicinity. It seemed to be looking at me, though. With most of its eyes. It did have a humongous amount of eyes. Kind of like fly eyes.

DOUG. Ewwww.

JANNA. I mean, it's hard to tell exactly what fly eyes are looking at.

DOUG. On second thought, this does not sound like an angel. Maybe you had an alien encounter.

JANNA. Aren't they supposed to be the same thing? That's what Van Damme thought, you know.

DOUG. Jean Claude Van Damme saw aliens? In what karate movie?

JANNA. No, the other guy. "Chariots of the Gods." Who saw all the crop circles from the air in South America and stuff.

DOUG. Erik Von Daniken.

JANNA. Whoever. Angels and aliens are manifestations of the same spiritual impulse. Even Carl Jung believed that. They show up at particular times when people are predisposed to look.

DOUG. Well, I don't want to look at a fly-eyed creature who smells like pot roast, thanks. If that doesn't turn you into a vegetarian, nothing will.

JANNA. But it was awe-inspiring. It radiated some kind of shimmering. I was magnetized to its every flutter. And its voice was—thrilling. Like the bass turned up real high in a Rolling Stones song.

DOUG. Bad sign! Sounds demonic.

JANNA. Don't be so literal. It wasn't *really* a sound I was hearing in my ears, it was deeper. Everything was really quiet—almost a buzzing quiet—and then when it said: "Behold,"

DOUG. "I bring you tidings of great joy"—

JANNA. No, that wasn't it.

DOUG. "which shall be to all people."

JANNA. Nope.

DOUG. "I bring you a miracle."

JANNA. No.

DOUG. "A mystery."

JANNA. Better. That was more the sense of it, anyway.

DOUG. "Behold, I bring you a mystery. And his name
is—"

JANNA. There wasn't a "his" in it.

DOUG. No gender.

JANNA. If there *was* a gender, and I'm not really sure
there was, it was female.

DOUG. Come on.

JANNA. I distinctly got the impression it was, sort of, female.

DOUG. Oh, a *feminist* angel-slash-alien.

JANNA. Don't be so difficult!

DOUG. You were projecting femaleness on it. It was talking,

JANNA. humming.

DOUG. It was humming at you,

JANNA. Buzzing, more like a buzz.

DOUG. *Buzzing* at you—shoot, it really *does* sound like a
fly! Maybe it's an insectoid angel.

JANNA. Doug.

DOUG. You heard it buzzing at you and so you assumed
it was talking about a female mystery.

JANNA. Well, why would it tell me about a *male* mystery,
Mister Big Shot! Why would it bother telling me about
a mystery that I was excluded from? To make me jealous?

DOUG. Maybe it wasn't even talking to you. Maybe it
was a general revelation and you're merely its tempo-
rary custodian. The Pot Roast Chronicles, as revealed to—

JANNA. You always turn everything into a joke. Every-thing you can't understand. It becomes something to make fun of, so you can tag it and capture it and mount it. Everything is just this stuffed punch line.

(A wounded silence.)

DOUG. I think you're making an awful lot out of a freaky dream.

JANNA. Am I? So why is my revelation any less valid than Saint John's? Tell me that. Because there's no pes-tilence or death or threats in it? Because you can't hold it over somebody's head and scare the crap out of them to manipulate their behavior? I could have had a revela-tion like that, no problem. Those are a dime a dozen, just do a little channel surfing.

DOUG. It isn't much of a message. "Behold."

JANNA. It's terse.

DOUG. Ambiguous, I'd say.

JANNA. Pithy. Right to the point.

DOUG. You don't think there was another part, and he got—

JANNA. It wasn't a he!

DOUG. She. It. And it got interrupted before you know what you're supposed to behold?

JANNA. I dunno. It had a feeling of perfect completeness. With the buzzing-humming, and the tingling...

DOUG. What tingling?

JANNA. The way all my muscles were tingling.

DOUG. You didn't say that before. Anything about tingling.

JANNA. I didn't?

DOUG. No.

JANNA. Well, that was part of it. Like all my muscles were on fire—well, no, more like woken up. I hadn't even known they were asleep, but they were suddenly all awake and alive now, kind of like—

DOUG. What?

JANNA. Kind of like right after a monster orgasm—crossed with a really really big hit of mushrooms.

DOUG. Mushrooms?

JANNA. Like, you know, magic mushrooms, sort of like peyote, only...

DOUG. What do you know from mushrooms?

JANNA. Doug. Duh.

DOUG. You took drugs? Major psychedelics?

JANNA. Well...

DOUG. When did you do that?!

JANNA. I mean, come oh, it was college, the '70s, you shouldn't *have* to ask.

DOUG. Well, there you go. Drug flashback! You're having a—

JANNA. See, this is why I never told you. Now every time I fart it will get explained away as a drug flashback.

DOUG. I can't believe you didn't tell me this. Who knows about this?

JANNA. Oh, for heaven's sake, Doug, you make it sound like I was shooting smack. I tripped a couple of times, okay. Why? Are you secretly planning to run for state representative or auditor or dogcatcher or something? I wouldn't want my lurid past to trip you up.

DOUG. I can't say I like where this is going.

JANNA. All those drug-induced sexual escapades. The orgies. The three-ways. You know. (*DOUG is silent. Looks hurt. A beat.*) Sorry. I got kind of carried away.

DOUG. Our life is kind of boring, huh.

JANNA. Forget it.

DOUG. "Behold." I bring you a mystery. Now that's exciting.

JANNA. I was just—trying to describe the feeling.

DOUG. Tingling.

JANNA. The *feeling*. Why it was so...so... *(Falls silent.)*

DOUG. Complete.

JANNA. Why it felt... Why I felt... *(On the verge of tears.)* Like my body had been a fist that I didn't even know was a fist, and suddenly it was just...an open hand. Ready for...something.

(Silence.)

DOUG. It sounds great. Really. If something could make me feel like that, I'd...I wouldn't even mind about all the, you know. Eyes.

JANNA. There were an awful lot of them.

DOUG. "Behold." About seeing, maybe.

JANNA. Or even looking. Looking and seeing aren't the same thing.

(Beat. DOUG pats JANNA's hand.)

DOUG. "He that hath eyes—let him see."

(They look at each other—a beat—then they stare out at a slowly growing light.)

END OF PLAY

SOME FISH

By
Eric Berlin

Some Fish premiered in "An All Day Sucker Marathon," produced by The LAB at Circle in the Square Downtown, New York City, 1996. The play was directed by Guy Giarrizzo and featured Richard Hughs and G.R. Johnson.

CHARACTERS

FATHER
SON: About 15 years old.

SETTING: A fishing stream or pond.
TIME. The present.

SOME FISH

AT THE CURTAIN: *FATHER and SON are fishing. Long silence. SON looks morose.*

FATHER *(slowly)*. And there's some fish have gills on the inside. On the inside. They suck in the water. They extract the oxygen. All kinds of fish. Some fish ain't nothing but bone. Just bone. And some, skin stretched over the bones like tissue paper, stretched tight, and you can see right through. That fish don't need gills at all, water goes right through, it *seeps* through and the nutrients and the minerals in the water, they're absorbed and the fish can live. Something like that can live. It is able to live.

SON. I have homework.

FATHER. You have homework, but I am talking. Some fish live down on the floor of the water and they bury themselves. Bury themselves in the ocean floor. *(Pause.)*

SON. And they get minerals...?

FATHER. They don't! They stay there and they die. Or they *don't* stay there and they die. They swim up for a moment and they're eaten! Either way, they die. So they stay there, buried. And they live longer. There's some fish that you can't tell which part is the head. Looks like they've got, maybe, six heads, each pointing in a different direction, but only one is the real head. Makes it real tricky to sneak up on.

SON. But it swims.

FATHER. Of course it swims! It's a fish!

SON. So it *swims*. So, so, you know which is the head. *(Pause.)* From which way it's *going*.

FATHER. That doesn't tell you nothing. Nothing can be gleaned from this.

SON. But...

FATHER. There's some fish can swim backwards! Right backwards. So maybe that's the head coming to you or maybe that's the head swimming away. You just don't know. Fish don't take chances with fish like that. Do you see what I'm saying to you, Son? Are you seeing this?

SON. There's different fishes.

FATHER. There are! All sorts! And just because you're a fish with your head on backwards, doesn't mean you don't belong in the sea!

SON. Okay.

FATHER. Do you understand that?

SON. Yes, Dad. *(Long pause.)* I have homework.

FATHER. There's some fish that—you know what they do?

SON. Dad.

FATHER. They don't bite other fish or swallow 'em whole. They just *bully* them. Knock them into rocks or...chase them away. Just chase them every time they come near. Ugly, bullying fish. These fish exist. And then the other fish, the smaller fish, their victims, they finally say, "Okay. You win. You are the better fish." And then they are eaten. *(Pause.)*

SON. They "say" this?

FATHER. What?

SON. They say this? Out loud?

FATHER *(angry)*. They don't *say* it. They're underwater! Even if they could speak, they open their mouths and they are instantly filled with water! And besides that, fish need their mouths for other things. Eating and breathing. Even if they could speak, there would be no time to speak. So of course they don't say it. They use, what they call, body language. *(Pause.)* Or, there are some fish that don't need to see body language. They just *know* how another fish feels. They may know it better than that fish itself. There are some fish just *know*. Do you see, Son?

SON. All right, Dad.

FATHER. Don't "all right Dad" me. Whaddaya, not believe me?

SON *(he doesn't)*. I believe you.

FATHER. You better! You better believe this, Son: There's all kinds of fishes and they all belong where they are. *(Pause.)* All kinds. And, and, and, that's what makes this land *great*.

SON. Dad, we're not catching any.

FATHER. No, there's something else to tell you. Fish. All fish have their roles, Son. There's all kinds of fish and they all have something to do. They each have a purpose, every one of them. There's fish that what they do is, what they do is, they open up oysters. They are put into the sea to do this. Open up oysters. And there are fish that make sure the ocean floor is free from debris. And they don't take each other's jobs down there. They do what they're told. That's right. *(Pause.)* And, and, what happens when an oyster-opening fish dies? What do you think happens?

SON. To the oysters?

FATHER. To the *environment*. To the…*situation*.

SON. I, I don't know.

FATHER. The oysters stay *closed*. That's what. That's the end of the story. *(Pause.)* Up here on land, we find someone else to open that oyster. You know?

SON. Yes.

FATHER. Up here, the *job* does not go away simply because of, of... the job must still get *done*.

SON. I know.

FATHER. Down below they adapt to such an event. Up here we have no such luxury.

SON. I know.

FATHER. The job up here must still get done. Every job. And if that means someone has two jobs, then that's what that means. The fish cannot do this. They are only able to do their one job. But here we must take on more if we must.

SON. Dad, I don't think there's fish in this lake. I've never even seen anyone fishing here.

FATHER. You know everything then, do you? Fifteen years old and you know every square inch of, of, of...

SON. No.

FATHER. Well, let's just wait. Let's just sit here. Let's just wait.

SON. It's just, I have homework.

FATHER. How often do I take you fishing, huh?? How often do we get this chance??

SON. I'm sorry.

FATHER. You are entirely my responsibility now. And until you are old enough to decide otherwise, if I say we're fishing then by gosh we're fishing.

SON. I'm sorry.

FATHER. It's like your mom said to you, to be sure you listen to me. Isn't that right?

SON. Yes.

FATHER. That's right. *(Pause.)* So we're gonna sit here and fish. And *talk.* Your mother always said I never *spoke* to you but that's what I'm doing now.

SON *(low).* There's just no fish, that's all.

FATHER. I used to say to her, "*You* talk to him, what do *I* need to talk to him for?" She was better at it. Wasn't she?

SON. Yes.

FATHER. Yes she was. And that was fine. But now I see what I have to do. And so here we are fishing, *right*??

SON. Yes.

FATHER. Yesiree. And you're learning something.

SON. Learning?

FATHER. About fish, Son, about fish!

SON. Oh.

FATHER. I'm telling you about fish. There's some fish lay a million eggs. And they all hatch at once, and all the babies swim out to sea. And nobody ever hears from those fish again. But those fish are out there. They're all out there. Swimming. And there's fish that when they die, no one notices because there's so many other fish out there anyway. *(Pause.)* Your mama, she was a better person than me. Deserved better. Deserved better than you and me combined. But better never came along and so she settled for me. Strong woman! Your mama was a strong woman! Another woman, pregnant or no, would have cast me off! My no-good-nothing. But your mama settled in for the long haul with me because that's what she knew she had to do. You were coming, you know. And I said, if you can do this, then by God so can I, but we have to understand our *jobs.* I don't know nothing about babies, nothing about kids. I will *provide* and you will *care.* *(Pause.)* That was the system, that was the system my own parents had on the table. *(Pause.)* But now ... But that won't work now, will it, Son. *(Beat.)* I say, *will it?*

SON. Yes.

FATHER. *Yes??*

SON. I mean, no, no.

FATHER. Of course not! I know that. You're just a boy, you need, what do you call, human *contact. (Beat.)* Social, what do you call, installment of *values. (Beat.)* That was your mom's job, you know, we had a deal! She has, through no true fault of her own, but nonetheless, she has abandoned her fair share of things! Now what am I to do about that! Send you on your way? Of course not. But she dropped her end of the rope. And now what. So it falls to me. I can see that. And so. *Contact.* And values. Fine. And learning! Today, fish. Tomorrow, I don't know, maybe cars. Cars or something. But today, fish. There's fish out there that are sophisticated, they know just what those other fish are going to do in a situation. And so they are able to engage in strategies. To catch the other fish. Of course, when *those* fish meet *other* fish of equal sophistication, well then, they each have a problem, don't they?

SON. Yes. You don't have to teach me about fish. It's okay.

FATHER. No, Son, it's what I'm here for. So those fish of equal sophistication, they wind up engaging in warfare. And other fish just plain get out of the way. *(Pause.)* And there's some fish, they want to be like us. They want to be a family. But they don't know how. They're just fish. So they don't know how.

(Pause. They sit there. LIGHTS fade.)

END OF PLAY

SURRENDER

By

Barry Brodsky

CHARACTERS

LOUISE: In her 20s, professionally dressed.
MARY: In her 20s, professionally dressed.
DAVID: In his 40s, shabbily dressed.

SETTING: A sparsely furnished room. A table with two
chairs. A coffee pot and a few cups are on the table.

TIME: The present.

SURRENDER

AT THE CURTAIN: *LOUISE is seated at the table, sipping coffee. MARY is standing, staring offstage.*

LOUISE. What is it?
MARY. Come here and see.

(LOUISE joins MARY and stares off for a short moment.)

LOUISE. Should we call the police?
MARY. I am the police.
LOUISE. Then go cut him down.

(MARY exits quickly, LOUISE returns to table and sips cup. A thud is heard offstage. A moment later MARY re-enters, pushing DAVID ahead of her. Disoriented, DAVID falls to the floor.)

MARY. His eyes were about to pop out of his head.
LOUISE. Want a cup of coffee, David?

(DAVID tries to answer, can't talk, so he nods his head.)

MARY. Why'd you go and do something like that?
LOUISE. Let him sip some coffee.

(DAVID sits up, sips some coffee.)

MARY. You ready to go now?

LOUISE. There's no rush.

MARY. Yes there is.

DAVID *(getting up)*. I thought you were helping me.

LOUISE. I am helping you.

DAVID. I want another cup.

LOUISE. We know you're nervous.

DAVID. Just one more cup first.

MARY. They're expecting us.

DAVID. Just take a couple minutes.

LOUISE. We really shouldn't keep them waiting anymore.

DAVID. A few minutes won't matter.

MARY. Let's go!

(DAVID sits, begins to weep. He weeps softly for a moment.)

LOUISE. I guess a few minutes won't matter.

MARY. A few minutes.

DAVID *(composing himself)*. I hope I'm doing the right thing here.

LOUISE. Of course you are.

DAVID. You made it sound so sensible.

LOUISE. It is sensible, David.

DAVID. I'm not sure anymore.

LOUISE. Tell him it's sensible.

MARY. It's sensible.

LOUISE. More sense than hanging yourself.

MARY. A lot more sense.

LOUISE. Put your life in order.

DAVID. I don't know.

LOUISE. Walk around with your head held high.

DAVID. Easy for you to say.

MARY. Oh, be a man for once in your life.

DAVID. Easy for you to say!

LOUISE. Be proud of yourself.

DAVID. I feel sick!

MARY *(beat)*. They're waiting.

DAVID. Can I drink my coffee please?

LOUISE. Who's stopping you?

DAVID. It isn't easy you know.

LOUISE. I know.

MARY. I know.

DAVID. You don't know nothing.

LOUISE. I've done things that weren't easy.

DAVID. Like what?

MARY. Yeah, like what?

LOUISE *(thinks a moment)*. I passed the bar exam.

MARY. On your fourth try.

DAVID. Fifth!

LOUISE. It's no easier than the first.

DAVID. You both got easy lives.

LOUISE. Being a lawyer is not easy.

DAVID. Why not?

LOUISE. Well, you have to enjoy talking.

DAVID. I'd hate a job where I had to talk a lot.

LOUISE. There you go.

DAVID *(to MARY)*. But you got an easy job.

MARY *(angrily)*. You think being a cop's easy?

DAVID. Sure it is.

MARY. I have to report to work at six o'clock every morning!

DAVID. I hate getting up early.

MARY. And I have to fill out forms at least two hours a day!

DAVID. Oh God, I'd hate that.

LOUISE. David, living's all about learning to do things you hate to do.

DAVID. Nobody ever taught me how to do that.

LOUISE. Should we tell him?

MARY. I don't know.

DAVID. Please?

LOUISE. Might make things easier for him to take.

MARY. Why's he so special?

DAVID. Ple-ee-ase??

LOUISE. Make it easier to get him out of here?

MARY. All right, all right.

LOUISE. We'll explain it to you, David.

DAVID. Oh thank you, thank you both.

MARY. Pipe down.

LOUISE. When you have to do something you don't want to do...

DAVID. Like go with you now.

MARY. Exactly.

LOUISE. ...just pretend you're doing something else.

DAVID. Yeah?

LOUISE. When I go to court, I pretend I'm going somewhere else.

DAVID. You do the same thing?

MARY. I'm always pretending I'm somewhere else.

DAVID. Works?

LOUISE. Like a charm.

MARY. Guaranteed.

DAVID. Think I could try it?

LOUISE. I don't see why not.

DAVID. What do I do?

LOUISE. Where you going?

DAVID. You know where I'm going.

MARY. She means pretend, stupid.

DAVID. Oh, uh, uh, I'm going to get married!

LOUISE. Good!

DAVID. To a beautiful girl.

LOUISE. You lucky guy.

DAVID *(dreamily)*. A beautiful girl who's just crazy about me.

LOUISE. Where you going for a honeymoon?

DAVID. Taking a cruise around the world.

MARY. You can't afford that.

DAVID. Well, she's loaded.

LOUISE. Living off your wife?

MARY. Scumbag.

DAVID. Not exactly living off her.

MARY *(pushes him)*. I wonder what she sees in you anyway.

DAVID. I got a lot of good features.

LOUISE. Forget the wedding.

MARY. Yeah, forget about it.

DAVID. I thought you were helping me.

LOUISE. I am helping you.

DAVID. Can I try another one?

LOUISE. Go for it.

DAVID. You two are taking me to a new job!

MARY. What kind of job?

DAVID. Executive job.

LOUISE. Ah, the best kind.

DAVID. With my own office.

MARY. Your own secretary?

DAVID. Two secretaries.

LOUISE. Company credit card?

DAVID. Company limo.

MARY. Forty-second floor?

DAVID (*dancing around the stage*). Air-conditioned!

LOUISE. Bottle of Scotch in the bottom right desk drawer?

MARY. Carpets on the floor?

LOUISE. Dental insurance?

DAVID (*as if hanging them as he speaks*). Lots of pictures on the wall.

MARY. Did he say executive?

DAVID (*sing-songy*). Music in the elevator.

LOUISE. I think so.

MARY. Who'd hire him for an executive job?

LOUISE. Who hired you, David?

DAVID (*snapping out of it*). Why, the company hired me.

MARY. Must've lied on his application.

DAVID. What are you talking about?

MARY. You never did an honest day's work in your whole life.

DAVID. What's that got to do with being an executive?

LOUISE. You do have to have the proper training.

MARY. A good education.

LOUISE. Not to mention the right connections.

DAVID. Hey, I thought you were helping me.

LOUISE. I am helping you.

DAVID. All right, forget the job.

MARY. It's long forgotten.

DAVID. We're going to the ball game.

MARY. Ball game?

LOUISE. What ball game?

DAVID. The baseball game.

LOUISE. There's no baseball game today.

DAVID. I'm pretending!

LOUISE. You have to pretend football.

MARY. No, hockey!

DAVID. I hate football and hockey.

LOUISE. It's not baseball season.

DAVID. I'm pretending it's baseball season.

LOUISE. I said pretend you're going somewhere else, not pretend it's another time of year.

MARY (pushes him). Pay attention to the rules, David.

DAVID. But why can't I pretend two things at once?

LOUISE. That just complicates matters.

DAVID (beat). You're awful smart, Louise.

MARY. She's a lawyer.

DAVID. Me too!!

LOUISE. You too what?

DAVID. I'm going to argue a really big case today.

LOUISE. What kind of case?

DAVID. My client's up for the electric chair.

MARY. Hope he's made out his will!

DAVID. Hey!

MARY. Notified his next of kin.

DAVID. Louise!

LOUISE. Don't be a lawyer, David.

DAVID. I thought you were helping me.

LOUISE. I AM HELPING YOU!!!

DAVID. Then you think of something.

LOUISE. I thought you'd never ask.

DAVID. And make it good.

MARY. I got one.

DAVID. I want Louise to think of one.

MARY. Try mine first.

LOUISE. No, I got one.

DAVID. I'll try yours, Louise.

LOUISE. They're waiting for you.

DAVID. Who's waiting for me?

LOUISE. At the hospital.

DAVID. I thought we were pretending!

MARY. Told you to try mine.

LOUISE. We told them we'd be bringing you in today.

DAVID. Aren't you the dedicated public servants.

LOUISE. You should be very happy.

DAVID. I don't want to see no doctors again, Louise.

LOUISE. Oh, it's not just doctors waiting for you.

DAVID. Who else?

LOUISE. Television!

DAVID. You're kidding.

MARY. Cable TV?

LOUISE. Network!

DAVID. For me?

MARY. You're big news, David.

DAVID. I never would have imagined.

LOUISE. Lots of people are expecting you to go back today, David.

DAVID (sips cup). This coffee's cold.

LOUISE. I told them to have a fresh pot ready when we got there.

MARY. Ready to go?

DAVID. I need to get my hat.

LOUISE. Where is it?

DAVID. In my bedroom.

MARY. Hurry it up.

DAVID. I will. *(Beat.)* You know, I think that little talk we had really worked. I was always wondering what the secret was. Why I just couldn't seem to get things right, no matter what I tried I always just screwed up. Now I get it. I know what I wasn't doing. Pretend I'm someone else. Thank you, Louise. Thank you for helping me.

LOUISE. Think nothing of it.

(DAVID exits. MARY sips the coffee and makes a face. LOUISE fiddles with the cup on the table.)

MARY. He can talk, that one.

LOUISE. So what was yours, anyway?

MARY. Circus.

LOUISE. Clown?

MARY. Man shot from a cannon.

LOUISE. He'd have liked that.

MARY *(beat)*. Taking him an awful long time to get his hat.

LOUISE. Probably misplaced it.

MARY. I wonder what he meant with that long speech of his.

LOUISE. Although, I can't say I ever saw David wearing a hat.

MARY. You don't think he'd try to make a break for it, do you?

LOUISE *(thinks for a second, gets up)*. David?

MARY. Sit down.

LOUISE. I want to look for him.

MARY. That's my job. *(MARY stares off.)*

LOUISE. What is it?

MARY. Come here and see.

(LOUISE joins MARY and stares off for a short moment.)

LOUISE. Should we call the police?
MARY. I am the police.
LOUISE. Then go cut him down.

(MARY exits very slowly. LOUISE returns to table and sips coffee. A thud is heard offstage.)

END OF PLAY

COVERS

By
Sandra Perlman

Covers was a finalist in the 1992 Actors Theatre of Louisville National Ten-Minute Play Contest and premiered at the Cleveland Play House in 1994. It was also produced by CollaborAction Theatre in Chicago in 2000.

CHARACTERS

PAULETTE: A pregnant teenager.
TONYA: A pregnant teenager.

SETTING: A halfway house for pregnant teens. Two cots with a nightstand and a light between them.

TIME: The present.

COVERS

AT THE CURTAIN: *There is just the starkness of two cots next to each other in the dark with two figures underneath the blankets. A small table with a lamp sits between them.*

PAULETTE *(pause)*. You asleep?

TONYA *(pause)*. Nah.

PAULETTE *(turning on the light)*. How come you got your head under the covers?

TONYA. I've been sleeping with my head under the covers since I can remember...maybe before.

PAULETTE. Even when it's hot?

TONYA. Uh-huh.

PAULETTE. I hate sheets. I take the top one and roll it to the end of the bed so nobody sees 'cause I know we're suppose to keep the bed all together like we're given it, so every morning when I get up I roll it back on again, but I hate sheets on top of me. I just like the blanket. Close to my skin, 'specially when it's real soft and has a satin ribbon on the edge like this one. But I hate scratchy blankets. Like those dark army things people are always giving away. You can see why they give them away because they don't feel good next to your skin. You asleep?

TONYA *(shuts off the light)*. No!

PAULETTE. Well how can you breathe with your head under there?

TONYA. I leave a little air hole like they do on a submarine.

PAULETTE. On a submarine? You ever been on a submarine?

TONYA. When my mother's sister died and we had to take the Greyhound all the way back to Philadelphia, one of my cousins, Julius, he took me down to see this submarine. I never met any boy like Julius. He talked quiet, knew all about the constellations in the sky and said he was goin' to college some day.

PAULETTE. I wouldn't want to be locked up in a box under the water. No, I don't even like putting my head under the water to wash the soap out and I never did learn to swim. You ever seen the ocean?

TONYA. Uh-huh.

PAULETTE. I saw a river, a lake and a pond, but not the ocean.

TONYA. Ocean's salty like pumpkin seeds. And it gets all bubbling when it comes in like the soap you put into the water when you're the first one to take a bath.

PAULETTE. Like pumpkin seeds?

TONYA. I just love the ocean.

PAULETTE. I couldn't use bubble bath since I was the last one in the water and it wasn't very nice. But sometimes, when I said I was too sick to go to school, I stayed home all alone, put some pink dish soap in the tub and sat all day.

TONYA. I took some bubbles in once but it made me and my other sister, Clarese, itch down in our privates so hard my mama said we couldn't use it ever again.

PAULETTE (turns off the light and goes to bed). You sleep with your head under the covers when you're with a boy?

TONYA (*jumps up and turns on the light*). I've never been with a boy all night long!

PAULETTE. Sorry. (*TONYA goes back to her bed.*) Where did you do it?

TONYA. Sometimes standing in a closet.

PAULETTE. Well that doesn't sound so good.

TONYA. Well where did you!

PAULETTE. Sometimes in a bed, but real fast before anybody came home. And I always used the top sheet then.

TONYA. Once on top of a washing machine.

PAULETTE. Was it running?

TONYA. No, stupid. It was a laundromat and it was supposed to be closed, but it was the most private place in my whole life.

(*TONYA turns off the light and PAULETTE turns it back on.*)

PAULETTE. What kind of games did you play when you were little?

TONYA. Don't you ever sleep?

PAULETTE. You play house?

TONYA. No.

PAULETTE. Dolls?

TONYA. No.

PAULETTE. Baseball?

TONYA. I was real good at double dutch.

PAULETTE. Me, too! (*Pause.*) Were you ever hungry?

TONYA. Uh-huh.

PAULETTE. 'Til your stomach wouldn't stop.

TONYA. Uh-huh. Did you have a doctor that knew your name?

PAULETTE. No. Did you have a daddy?

TONYA. For a while. You?

PAULETTE. For a while. My mama yelled a lot right after he left. Then she got so quiet she hardly moved. White blue sick is what the neighbors called it, and she never said my daddy's name out loud again.

TONYA. I was the mama since I was twelve, but I didn't like it so much.

PAULETTE. I hated the hard parts like cleaning and washing and cooking, but I liked the woman part.

TONYA. Yeah, like when everyone thinks you're all grown up.

PAULETTE. I'd take her clothes and pink lipstick with the rosy blush and I'd go out to the convenience to get the dinner...

TONYA. And the lunch...

PAULETTE & TONYA (*laughing together*). But no breakfast!!!

TONYA. Except doughnuts. But my mama said doughnuts ain't never breakfast, no matter how good they taste. (*Pause.*) How old they say you looked?

PAULETTE. Twenty-two on my next birthday.

TONYA. Said I looked close to twenty when I could still double dutch.

PAULETTE. After a while, I forgot how to jump rope.

TONYA (*pause*). How old were you when you did it for sure?

PAULETTE. Thirteen. Almost. For sure. But I'd been bleeding like a real woman for almost a year.

TONYA. How almost?

PAULETTE. Fourteen. You?

TONYA. Thirteen years and one day. Was it nice?

PAULETTE. He was real nice after. Bought me a whole big bottle of perfume.

TONYA. Was it your boyfriend?

PAULETTE. No.

TONYA. Me neither. *(Pause.)* Now I don't even think about it.

PAULETTE. You really do it standing up in a closet?

TONYA. No.

PAULETTE. I never did it in a bed, neither. *(Pause.)* You really saw the ocean?

TONYA. The sun setting just like it was a fried egg. Prettiest thing I ever saw. Tried to tell my mama, but she was crying so hard over her sister that she didn't hear me. Seems like every week she knew someone dying and she'd tell me she had a right to cry and I thought she did too. But still, I thought she'd stop sometime. But she didn't. Seems the only one who ever listened to me for sure was my brother, Louis. Louis listens to everything I say, but he doesn't speak, so I don't really know what he hears. There's something wrong with Louis, but nobody says nothing, and in the school they don't say nothin' either 'cause he's so good and they don't bother boys who are good. *(Pause.)* You have a brother?

PAULETTE. I got three sisters. I had a brother, twin brothers, but they died. They looked so much alike Mama had to put different suits on them in the coffin so she could know which one was which when she kissed them goodbye. But she only put up one stone since she said they wouldn't mind being together and, truthfully, she didn't even have the money for that one. She visits those babies every Sunday and sometimes I think she misses them more dead than me alive. At least that's what she says when she's mad at me—which is a lot. She doesn't mean it, though, I know she's just tired. She's just tired all the time. *(Pause.)* I promise I won't be tired when my baby comes along, not for one minute. No, I'll be there for my baby.

TONYA. Yeah, I won't be tired and I'll hear every word she says.

PAULETTE. You think your baby will sleep with its head under the blanket?

TONYA. Maybe.

PAULETTE. You think things get passed on?

TONYA. Maybe.

PAULETTE *(pause)*. You think sometime we could take our babies to see the ocean?

TONYA. I don't know, but I think it would make a big difference.

PAULETTE. You do?

TONYA. If they could see the ocean, they'd believe there was something else out there, something bigger and cleaner and better than what they see, and that would make them want to grow up to be bigger and cleaner and better than anything they ever see in this life. Yeah. I think it would make a big difference.

PAULETTE *(whispering)*. Yeah.

TONYA. Something worth believing in. *(TONYA turns off the light.)* Paulette?

PAULETTE. Yeah.

TONYA. You scared?

PAULETTE. Yeah.

TONYA. Real scared?

PAULETTE. Uh-huh.

TONYA. Me, too, but I couldn't say that with the light on. *(Pause.)* Do you think they'll let me take my special blanket to the hospital?

PAULETTE. I don't know...

TONYA. I brought it all the way from home.

PAULETTE. Well if they don't, I promise to bring it myself.

TONYA. You would do that for me?

PAULETTE. Yes. I would.

TONYA. Paulette?

PAULETTE. Yes?

TONYA. I keep my special blanket over my head so I can breathe in the warm air I just breathed out, which somehow makes me feel safe, you know, like a mama's breath when she's not crying, and she remembers who you are, and she loves you. *(Big sigh.)* I never told anyone such a personal thing before.

(PAULETTE turns on the light and stands next to TONYA's bed.)

PAULETTE. I'll never tell...

TONYA. Swear on your baby?

PAULETTE. I swear. *(Pause.)* You ever been to a hospital?

TONYA. One time when Louis got hit and took twenty stitches, once when my aunt died from the drugs, and when they put Mama in for two weeks 'cause she couldn't stop crying.

PAULETTE. Do you think it's gonna be the same?

TONYA. No, I don't think so. I don't think so at all.

PAULETTE *(doubles up)*. Oh my God!

TONYA. You gonna be sick?

PAULETTE. I don't know.

TONYA. You want to put your head under my blanket?

PAULETTE. No.

TONYA. You want me to call somebody?

PAULETTE. No, no, just don't leave me, please...

TONYA (*pause*). Better...? You better now?

PAULETTE (*pause*). If I die...

TONYA. No!

PAULETTE. Listen to me.

TONYA. I don't want to hear nothing about no dying!

PAULETTE. I gotta say it now... please. I got no one else in the whole world to say it to but you and I gotta say it right now before... (*Pause.*) If I die—

TONYA. —we're gonna live, Paulette. We are gonna live and we're gonna have two beautiful babies.

PAULETTE. Promise me you'll take my baby to see the ocean...

TONYA. We are gonna love those babies, Paulette. We are gonna take those babies to see the ocean, you hear me!

PAULETTE. Yes...

TONYA. Say you believe it!

PAULETTE. I believe it.

TONYA. Say it like you really believe it.

PAULETTE. ...whatever happens to me...

TONYA. ...I swear...

PAULETTE. ...my baby will see the ocean.

TONYA. ...I swear...

PAULETTE. ...my baby will see the ocean.

TONYA. ...whatever happens...

PAULETTE & TONYA. My baby will see the ocean.

(*Blackout.*)

END OF PLAY

ART CONTROL

By
Carter W. Lewis

Art Control premiered at the Festival of Ten, produced by SUNY Brockport, Brockport, N.Y., 2001. It received the Audience Choice Award.

CHARACTERS

FRANK
DONNA
WAITER
OFFICER JOE
PLAYWRIGHT
AUDIENCE MEMBER #1
AUDIENCE MEMBER #2
PROPS GUY

SETTING: A restaurant in Los Angeles.
TIME: The present.

ART CONTROL

AT THE CURTAIN: *FRANK and DONNA are sitting at a table in an L.A. restaurant. FRANK is eating his appetizer, DONNA has a salad in front of her but doesn't eat.*

FRANK. So then he pulls out a gun.

DONNA. Wait, wait, who pulls out a gun? The percussionist?

FRANK. No, no listen—you'll love this.

DONNA. I'm listening, I'm just hungry. The waiter didn't bring the vinaigrette. First he shoots ground pepper all over it, then no vinaigrette.

FRANK. The bruschetta is terrific.

DONNA. I'm glad.

FRANK. So he pulls out a gun.

DONNA. First violinist.

FRANK. What?

DONNA. OK, who pulls out the gun?!

FRANK. The conductor, the conductor!

DONNA. The conductor pulls out a gun?

FRANK. Now you've got it. And not just a gun, an AK forty-whatever, big mother bazooka-type thing.

DONNA. The conductor of the orchestra.

FRANK *(mouth full)*. This bruschetta is absolutely the best.

DONNA *(to a WAITER in the distance)*. Waiter. Excuse me.

FRANK. So he pulls out this cannon thing...

DONNA. Did anyone else have a gun?

FRANK. You're missing the point here.

DONNA. Well I'm getting a little lightheaded. Excuse me. Excuse me. Excuse me. Excuse me. Excuse me. Excuse me. Excuse me. Excuse me. Hello. *(Beat.)* Excuse me. Excuse me. Excuse me. Excuse me. Excuse me.

(WAITER comes to the table.)

DONNA. Could you please bring a little vinaigrette for my salad?

WAITER. Not my table.

DONNA. Yes, I know, but I can't find our waiter, and the lettuce and I are wilting.

WAITER. I'll try and find your waiter.

FRANK. The bruschetta is fabulous by the way.

WAITER. Everything's fresh is why. And if you check under the tomato, you'll find a little cilantro. Don't tell, but that's the real secret.

FRANK. Well, I'll be. That's what it is.

WAITER. You thought it was sesame oil, right? Everyone does. But it's cilantro. *And...* a little arugula.

FRANK. Good God!

DONNA. If you have time to discuss recipes, you have time to get the vinaigrette, right?

WAITER. I'll find your waiter. *(Exits.)*

FRANK *(mouth full)*. Fabulous. So, he's still conducting with his left hand and he's got this cannon thing in his right hand.

DONNA. So, did he shoot someone?

FRANK. No, no, no, Donna, please pay attention.

DONNA. I'm trying, Frank, I'm really trying. OK, OK, he pulls out a gun and what?

FRANK. Think back, remember how the story began.

DONNA. I was younger then, Frank. You started this story well before our waiter—who's obviously decided on a career change—forgot our drink order.

(WAITER enters with two plates of food.)

WAITER. Here we go, sorry about the wait. *(He puts the plates down.)* Jumbo Garlic Shrimp in Saffron and Veal Piccata with Asparagus spears. *(Without missing a beat, picks them back up.)* Ooopsy-boom, my mistake, wrong table. *(Exits.)*

FRANK. That smelled terrific! Didn't that smell terrific?

DONNA. So, the conductor has a gun!

FRANK. Right. Yes. And not just a gun, really, I mean it's...

DONNA. A cannon! A big mother AK forty-seven bazooka-like cannon!

FRANK. Honey, why not just eat it without the dressing.

DONNA. Who does he shoot, Frank, just tell me who he shoots.

FRANK. Well, that's just it. He doesn't shoot anyone.

DONNA. No one?

FRANK. Are you ready?

DONNA. Yes.

FRANK. Are you ready for this? Are you really ready?

DONNA. Yes, Frank, I'm ready.

FRANK. It's the "1812 Overture." *(Beat.)*

DONNA. This weapon is a musical instrument?

FRANK. Yes. You know. Duhn da da da da dum, boom boom. On the boom booms he fires the thing, straight through the sound shell. Shatters the damn thing. Plaster and wood comes raining down on everybody. The audience goes berserk!

DONNA. Well, I should think.

FRANK. And that's not all, the entire orchestra is packing!

DONNA. No.

FRANK. Yes. Right at the finale, they all stand and start shooting their guns in the air. Nobody's playing a lick of music anymore. Standing ovation, security guards give it a twenty-one-gun salute, the place is in chaos, three birds fall out of the sky dead.

DONNA. Incredible.

FRANK. Never seen anything like it. There's one orchestra's gonna pull some mucho funding dollars next year, let me tell you.

DONNA. Those sound shells are expensive.

(The WAITER approaches with vinaigrette.)

DONNA. Ah, here, finally. Thank you thank you thank you.

WAITER. This is for table six.

DONNA. No, I've been asking for vinaigrette for twenty minutes now.

WAITER. But I'm not your waiter.

DONNA. Well get to know me, goddamnit! Now I must insist that that is *my* vinaigrette.

WAITER. It's for table six. I've got two customers waiting.

DONNA. They just got their salads didn't they? I mean just moments ago, right? There's no need to *rush* the vinaigrette to them.

WAITER. I'm sorry, ma'am, I'll try and find...

DONNA *(pulls a pistol from her purse)*. Put the vinaigrette down.

WAITER. Now look, ma'am, there's no need to...

DONNA. Put. The. Vinaigrette. Down.

FRANK *(still eating, mouth full)*. I'd put it down.

WAITER. All right. All right. *(Cautiously puts vinaigrette on the table.)* There you go. Put a little on your salad. And I'll take it over to six.

(DONNA doesn't move.)

FRANK. Just put a little on, and he'll...

DONNA. It stays.

WAITER. OK. Okaaaay.

(DONNA warily picks vinaigrette up and is about to pour it on her salad. The WAITER pulls a gun from his vest and points it at her.)

WAITER. OK, put the vinaigrette back on the tray.

DONNA. But I haven't used any yet.

WAITER. I'm afraid that's no longer an option.

DONNA *(turns her gun back on the WAITER. Stalemate)*. I said, I haven't used any yet. *(Beat.)*

FRANK. Look, look, why don't we settle this like grown-ups. Just let her use a little of the vinaigrette. Look, here, I'll serve as the intermediate. I'll do it myself. A little in the coffee cup here and...

WAITER. I'm afraid I can't let you do that, sir.

FRANK. This is all very reactionary, young man, this is not a drug cartel, it's a Bibb salad.

WAITER. It's gone a little beyond that, sir.

FRANK (*pulls a gun from his suit jacket, stands, points it at the WAITER's head*). OK, you're oh so right, it's gone well beyond that. How's that feel? You like that? What do you think of your precious little vinaigrette now?

WAITER. Stay calm, sir.

FRANK. I'm very calm. I've got my appetizer and it's fabulous. OK, honey … go ahead, pour.

DONNA (*with her gun still on the WAITER, she pours. Taunting. They are in a three-way with guns*). Ooooh, look at all that lovely vinaigrette. Just look at it.

FRANK. Pour big, baby. Pour big.

DONNA (*pouring*). Yeaaaaaaaaaaaah.

WAITER. Look, dammit, leave a little for table six.

(*OFFICER JOE enters in full LAPD uniform. No gun.*)

OFFICER. All right, all right. Everybody stay calm. What have we got, Tommy?

WAITER. What do you think?

OFFICER. Looks like a little condiment rage.

WAITER. And, Joe, table six is on edge. It's the vinaigrette.

OFFICER. It's always the vinaigrette. Folks, why don't we lower the weapons, OK?

DONNA. Hey, we're the customers here.

WAITER. She pulled first, Joe.

OFFICER. Ma'am, let me see the gun.

DONNA. This salad has been sitting here for a full half hour. What was I supposed to do?

FRANK. Should of ordered the bruschetta.

OFFICER. The bruschetta's terrific here.

DONNA. I just wanted a salad! And why should I listen to you, you don't even have a gun.

OFFICER. We at the LAPD have concluded guns to be somewhat ineffectual.

FRANK. You don't carry a gun?

OFFICER. None of us do. You see...there was a study done, the results of which indicated overwhelmingly that criminals are more easily subdued by a melodious but forceful voice.

FRANK. What?

OFFICER. Yeah...that's what the study concluded.

PLAYWRIGHT (*stands up in the audience and points a gun at the stage*). Wait, wait, wait, that's not what I wrote! Hold on. Everybody stop. Why doesn't the damn cop have a gun? I wrote a gun in the stage directions, doesn't anyone read the damn stage directions anymore?

DIRECTOR (*stands and points a gun at the PLAYWRIGHT*). They were excessive. As director, I made an artistic choice. I thought the gentler touch was appropriate. The cop is the only one who *doesn't* have a gun. There's relevance in that.

PLAYWRIGHT. But that's not what the play is meant to say. If you'd followed the text, it was about to head directly toward the gun issue and several stinging observations.

DIRECTOR. Stinging observations?

PLAYWRIGHT. Yes, stinging observations, yes.

DIRECTOR. I don't recall any stinging observations.

PLAYWRIGHT. They're subtle. But why do I for a moment think you'd understand that. Just look at the audience, they're punch drunk from you bashing them in the face with your ever-so-subtle subtextual fists.

DIRECTOR. I'm entitled to my own statement within the piece. You can't bar me from my rightful aesthetic participation.

PLAYWRIGHT. On the contrary, your big-knuckled fingerprints are all over it!

DIRECTOR. I'm trying to save this piece of drek, and this is the thanks I get.

AUDIENCE MEMBER #1 *(stands up behind the DIRECTOR, gun to the DIRECTOR's head)*. All right, enough, turn over the gun. I'm entitled to a piece of this.

DIRECTOR *(handing the gun to him/her)*. Who are you?

AUDIENCE MEMBER #1. I bought a ticket, that's who I am. I'm your audience, and I'm taking over. *(To AUDIENCE MEMBER #2 next to him/her.)* Here, why don't you keep this?

AUDIENCE MEMBER #2 *(holds up a gun)*. Got my own, thanks.

VOICE *(loudspeaker)*. Attention. May I have your attention? Would everyone please put their guns down!

DONNA *(ACTORS shield their eyes, look out)*. Who's that?

WAITER. Coming from the back there.

FRANK. Maybe it's the critic.

DONNA. They don't usually hang around this long.

VOICE. Put your guns down! Everyone put your guns down! *(ALL lower their guns.)* You, playwright, you, director, sit down!

PLAYWRIGHT. Who is it?

DIRECTOR. Board of Directors meddling as usual.

OFFICER JOE *(recognizes the person)*. Oh, damn. That's...

WAITER. You're right, it is!

DONNA. Who is it?

FRANK. It's the props guy.

(PROPS GUY comes down the aisle with a rifle pointed.)

PROPS GUY. OK, OK, you wanna know why the damn cop doesn't have a gun? This is a ten-minute play, right!? And the playwright wants six guns! Six guns for a stinking ten-minute play! Well, I found five, OK? Anybody got a problem with that. Oh yeah, and he wants them all to fire on cue. Didn't know that, did you!? Oh, yeah, the stupid play ends in mayhem. Big gooey-guts shootout, bloodpacks, sprayed bullets. Thinks it's a damn John Woo film. Well I found five! OK!? Everybody kick their guns to the middle here. All right. Go on. We are gonna do a play without a damn gun in it. Anybody got a problem with that?!

(ACTORS ad lib consent, favor.)

PLAYWRIGHT. Wait a minute.

PROPS GUY *(cocks rifle steps to edge of stage).* I said SIT DOWN, word boy! *(The PLAYWRIGHT sits.)* OK, OK. Like, everyone take one of these, OK? OK? Come on, everyone take one. This is gonna work, people. *(He passes out clickers.)* And you? *(To DONNA.)* I thought you were real good. So you read this. *(Gives DONNA a piece of paper.)* Go on. Everybody listen now! OK.

DONNA. Message. Guns are bad for literature. *(The PROPS GUY whispers in her ear.)* And music. If playwrights would stop putting guns in plays, then the audience could be sure they weren't at a movie. And if we didn't have so many guns in plays, when one did appear in a play, it would be like, a big surprise, and there would be a better chance that it would go off when it was supposed to. Signed... *(Glances at PROPS GUY.)* ... Sir Lawrence Olivier.

PROPS GUY. OK, OK. OK. *(Looks up at the sound booth.)* OK, play the tape. Everybody get ready. OK, OK, OK. Play it. *(The "1812 Overture" plays. When it gets to the "boom booms," the music stops, the PROPS GUY prompts and everybody clicks twice.)* OK. OK. Get ready now. Here it comes, big finish now. There! *(ALL click.)* Yeah. That's good. Here it comes again. Think integrity, people. Integrity! *(ALL click.)* Yeah! Now that's art. Yeah, we got some art happenin' here! Again!

(They continue, as the LIGHTS fade.)

END OF PLAY

THE SECRET OF OUR SEX LIFE

By

Richard Strand

The Secret of Our Sex Life was originally produced in 1992 by American Blues Theatre in Chicago as part of "Monsters II: Visiting Hours." The play featured Elaine Carlson and Scott Anderson, and was directed by Carmen Roman.

CHARACTERS

MR. WEDGEWORTH:
MRS. WEDGEWORTH: — A married couple.

SETTING: A bare stage, two chairs.
TIME: The present.

THE SECRET OF OUR SEX LIFE

AT THE CURTAIN: *MR. and MRS. WEDGEWORTH sit side by side. They speak to the AUDIENCE.*

MR. WEDGEWORTH. Every night, after dark, I walk the dog before I go to bed.

MRS. WEDGEWORTH. As if the dog needs help "walking."

MR. WEDGEWORTH. Okay. I let the dog wander. And I climb the white pine tree in our backyard.

MRS. WEDGEWORTH. My husband needs the time to be alone. And so do I. I use the time to do my twenty-minute workout.

MR. WEDGEWORTH. The branches on a white pine are very evenly spaced. I can climb it like a ladder. *(Pause.)*

MRS. WEDGEWORTH. My husband and I have not been intimate for a long time.

MR. WEDGEWORTH. It has been many years since we've had sex.

MRS. WEDGEWORTH. We share the same bed but we do not have sex.

MR. WEDGEWORTH. Or talk about sex.

MRS. WEDGEWORTH. We used to talk about sex—

MR. WEDGEWORTH. We used to, back when we first got married—

MRS. WEDGEWORTH. But we gave it up.

MR. WEDGEWORTH. We gave up talking about it and we gave up doing it.

MRS. WEDGEWORTH. And really, we are better off.

MR. WEDGEWORTH. The only thing talking ever did was make us self-conscious.

MRS. WEDGEWORTH. We were already self-conscious.

MR. WEDGEWORTH. We figured out, early on, that we were not good at sex.

MRS. WEDGEWORTH. I think I was afraid. And unsure of our goals.

MR. WEDGEWORTH. I was clumsy at it. I didn't really know what buttons to push.

MRS. WEDGEWORTH. And more often than not someone got hurt.

MR. WEDGEWORTH. One way or another. So we gave it up. *(Pause.)* Once, years ago, when we still talked about it, I asked her what there was about the way I made love that she liked. She thought. A very long time—long enough to be embarrassing. Long enough to make me wish I had not asked the question. And when she arrived at an answer...

MRS. WEDGEWORTH. ...I told him that the thing I liked best, was afterwards, when he was all finished, when he laid quietly beside me and held my hand.

MR. WEDGEWORTH. She liked it when I held her hand.

MRS. WEDGEWORTH. Dutifully, and forever afterwards, he held my hand when he was done. And, I liked it when he did. *(To MR. WEDGEWORTH.)* I really did.

MR. WEDGEWORTH. It was all the other stuff, the stuff before holding hands, that she didn't like. And, actually, neither did I.

MRS. WEDGEWORTH. He suggested to me once that I was not allowing myself to "let go." If I would just "let go," I would learn to enjoy it. And if *I* enjoyed it, *he* would enjoy it. So I tried to "let go."

MR. WEDGEWORTH. But, it turns out, it is hard to tell the difference between, "letting go," and, "taking a nap." At the height of passion I was forced to open my eyes to reassure myself that she had not left the room.

MRS. WEDGEWORTH. So, "letting go," wasn't the answer. I got an idea that I could make things better by initiating sex more often. I figured that if I had sex often enough, it would grow on me.

MR. WEDGEWORTH. She used to go crazy with animal passion at odd hours of the night. Without warning, she was on top of me, rocking. It scared me. I began to develop a sleeping disorder, fearing a nocturnal ambush.

MRS. WEDGEWORTH. It wasn't making things better, so I quit initiating sex.

MR. WEDGEWORTH. And, for the most part, so did I. We slept better.

MRS. WEDGEWORTH. There was one terrible night when things really started to unravel. He was biting my toes, apparently in search of a previously undiscovered erogenous zone, and I was staring at the room, trying not to see snakes in the wallpaper.

MR. WEDGEWORTH. Her mind was clearly elsewhere, and at the moment of insertion . ...

MRS. WEDGEWORTH. ... as soon as I became aware of him inside me ...

MR. WEDGEWORTH. ... as I was on the crest of my wave, the shoreline in sight ...

MRS. WEDGEWORTH. ... I said, "yuck."

MR. WEDGEWORTH. ... she said, "yuck."

MRS. WEDGEWORTH. Oh, God, if I could have taken it back.

MR. WEDGEWORTH. She said, "Yuck." Yuck!

MRS. WEDGEWORTH. I really had not meant to say it. It slipped out. I don't think I even really meant, "yuck." I think I meant something more like, "Oooo." Or "Mmmmm." But what I said was, "Yuck."

MR. WEDGEWORTH. Yuck.

MRS. WEDGEWORTH. There was no taking it back. There was nothing to be done. He rolled off me and lay on his back.

MR. WEDGEWORTH. I stared at the room, trying not to see bear traps in the wallpaper.

MRS. WEDGEWORTH. We drifted uncomfortably off to sleep.

MR. WEDGEWORTH. We have never spoken of that night.

MRS. WEDGEWORTH. It passed, uncommented upon. But it gave us perspective. We have a new outlook.

MR. WEDGEWORTH. Sex, we believe, is not for everyone.

MRS. WEDGEWORTH. But ending the story here would give you an incomplete picture. The other thing you gotta know about us is I'm sort of a fitness nut...

MR. WEDGEWORTH. ...and I'm not.

MRS. WEDGEWORTH. I belong to a fitness club...

MR. WEDGEWORTH. ...and I don't.

MRS. WEDGEWORTH. I have begged him to join. Only he's not interested. He won't even give it a try. He had never even set foot inside a health club until the day when my car was in for repairs, and he came to the club, just to pick me up.

MR. WEDGEWORTH. They don't allow nonmembers into the club. At least, not into the exercise area. But they did let me go to a second-level observation deck where you can order carrot juice and look down on the various exercise rooms.

I was astounded by what I saw. There were dozens of rooms and each room had dozens of magic exercise machines. Machines that pulsed and spun and whirred. Machines that tugged and flexed and stretched in perfect unison with their operators. I could not take my eyes off one particular and peculiar exercycle—a stationary bike with a video screen mounted between the handle bars. The woman riding wore a sleeveless red leotard and white gym shorts. Her blond hair was pulled back with a sweatband; the muscles in her arms and legs were spectacularly well defined. The video screen generated a pictogram of a country road which came toward her at a rate determined by her pedaling. The handlebar pulled her upper body back and forth slowly while her legs spun in tight circles. Her clothing gently massaged her as it tightened and relaxed. I was actually embarrassed to be looking at her.

I was falling in love. This was sex. Not sex like it really is, but like it ought to be. Raw, mechanical sex. Sex with rules and a purpose. Sex with a video destination. A man could not feel awkward or clumsy or ashamed with a woman like her.

I nearly collapsed when I realized that my specter of sex on an exercyle was my wife.

I tapped on the window. Not so much to get her attention; mostly I was testing to see if what I was watching was real.

MRS. WEDGEWORTH. I turned and saw him. But I pretended not to. I always get a better workout if I think someone is watching me. Knowing I was being watched by my husband made me—I can hardly believe it myself—I actually giggled.

I pedaled faster. I was giddy. I let go of the handlebars and, continuing to pedal, I stretched my arms over my head. I may not be great at sex, but there is nothing about my body I am ashamed of.

I shifted to a higher gear and pedaled so hard that the video image began to blur.

MR. WEDGEWORTH. She pointed her toes as she pedaled; she snapped her head with each backward thrust of the handle bars; she tightened her stomach and arched her back. She was a dancing automaton.

MRS. WEDGEWORTH. Pixilated trees whizzed by me at an ever-increasing rate. I was pushing too hard to keep my breathing regular.

MR. WEDGEWORTH. The screen was moving so fast, I worried she might have an accident. I had never seen her like this. So in her element. So at home. So able to, "let go." *(Pause.)*

And so, every night, I walk the dog. And I climb the white pine that grows in my backyard. I climb until I can peer through my own bedroom window.

MRS. WEDGEWORTH. I open the curtains, and I do my exercise routine. I stretch out, then I increase my heart rate to eighty percent of my maximum. I hold it there for twenty minutes. Afterwards, I take a shower, forgetting to draw the shower curtain.

MR. WEDGEWORTH. I watch her. I wrap my legs around the trunk of the tree; my face rests against the bark.

MRS. WEDGEWORTH. I dry myself off and I get into bed.

MR. WEDGEWORTH. I return to the house. I take a shower and wash sap from my cheek. And I get into bed with my wife.

MRS. WEDGEWORTH. And he holds my hand.

END OF PLAY

HOT WAX

By
Nancy Hanna

CHARACTERS

ANNIE: A shut-in.

PAIGE: A businesswoman who sells fine silks door to door to special customers.

SETTING: Annie's sitting-room in an urban high-rise apartment building. The room features numerous dusty, aged treasures.

TIME: The present.

HOT WAX

AT THE CURTAIN: *ANNIE is holding a blue silk scarf.*
   Studies it.

ANNIE. Nice. Something about it...
PAIGE. So...can we call it a sale? What do you think?
ANNIE *(holding it lightly)*. I can't.
PAIGE. You've been looking at it for a half an hour.
ANNIE. Have I?
PAIGE. Okay, so here, let me have it back. I've got to get
   going.
ANNIE. What?
PAIGE. Give it back, okay?
ANNIE. No. I didn't say I won't, I just said I can't...
   shouldn't. Give me a minute.
PAIGE. I don't have a minute. I don't have an hour. I'm
   out of time. Really.
ANNIE. Why are you always in a rush?
PAIGE. You're just one of the people I visit. You can't
   get out, so I come to you—to help you out.
ANNIE. You're always on your way somewhere...else.
PAIGE. It's not personal. Look, I have a business to run.
   If you don't want it someone else will.
ANNIE. You don't like me, do you?
PAIGE. Do we have to get personal?
ANNIE. This is personal. My life is very personal...to me.
PAIGE. Jean...
ANNIE. Personal is what makes it my life.
PAIGE. I think you've misinterpreted my visits.

ANNIE. Annie.

PAIGE. I don't come here just to visit. I have a business to run.

ANNIE. Annie. My name's Annie, not Jean.

PAIGE. I'm sorry. I knew that. I know that.

ANNIE. But you don't. No one here knows my name. I've lived here for twelve years. Why'd you call me Jean?

PAIGE. Now this is nothing "personal," Annie. I'd love to stay and visit, but I've got to push off now. If you don't want it, I'll just take it back. *(PAIGE takes the scarf from ANNIE.)* See there, now it's gone. No harm done. If you're lonely, maybe you could make some friends around here. Don't you have any family? Where are they?

ANNIE. Do I remind you of someone?

PAIGE *(packing up)*. No. Not that I can think of.

ANNIE. Who is Jean?

PAIGE. Jean? Oh let's see, how many Jeans do I know? I had a teacher named Jean. Blue jeans, of course.

ANNIE. My eyes are blue. That's it, my eyes remind you of blue jeans.

PAIGE. And my mother's name was Jean. Jean Carry to be exact.

ANNIE. Can't I have it back?

PAIGE. You don't look a thing like her.

ANNIE. I'll take it. I want it. It's a beautiful scarf.

PAIGE. Look, I've packed it all up. How about next week? I'll bring it by, next time.

ANNIE. Now. Unpack it, please. I don't care what it costs. What was she like?

PAIGE. Oh bother. *(Begins to unpack, looking for it.)* She was unremarkable...in every way. Except for her hands.

ANNIE. How much is it?

PAIGE. Eighty.

ANNIE. That's outrageous. What about her hands?

PAIGE. It's silk. Handpainted.

ANNIE. By whom? *(Referring to scarf.)* What about your mother's hands?

PAIGE. How should I know? They were always swollen, chafed.

ANNIE. My hands are nothing like that. Not a thing.

PAIGE. I didn't say they were, "Annie."

ANNIE. So aren't you going to tell me?

PAIGE. I told you, it's eighty dollars, handpainted.

ANNIE. By who? If it's French okay, if it's Taiwanese forget it.

PAIGE. It's French.

ANNIE. Oh yeah, right. Like I'm suppose to believe that.

PAIGE. Do you see the detailing? Look at the whimsy, not everyone can do that, and here it's signed: Madame O'Dell. Now eighty please. It's worth twice that.

ANNIE. Francs, pounds or dollars?

PAIGE *(icy)*. Dollars, please.

(ANNIE scrounges through handbags, drawers, jars to collect the money. She holds it out to PAIGE, PAIGE goes to take it. ANNIE pulls it back.)

ANNIE. Why were your mother's hands all swollen?

PAIGE. I couldn't say.

ANNIE. What do you mean?

PAIGE. I don't remember. Now I've got to be going. *(She looks toward ANNIE for the money.)*

ANNIE. I'm sure you do. Places to go, people to see. Friends, business associates, family... It's just I was wondering... there has to be a reason...

PAIGE. For what?

ANNIE. Why you called me Jean.

PAIGE. You're just like her...

ANNIE. I thought you said I wasn't a thing like her.

PAIGE. Can I have my money now?

(Standoff. ANNIE goes to the window.)

ANNIE *(leading PAIGE to tell about her mother)*. Yes, I like beautiful things. Yes, I can afford them. Lots of them. Enough to keep you in chocolate, keep your hands from becoming chafed... red... swollen. Maybe even enough for you to retire early.

PAIGE. What do you want to know?

ANNIE. Why your mother's hands were red and swollen.

PAIGE. She made candles. The wax burned her fingers.

ANNIE. Wow, really. Is she still alive?

PAIGE. No. She was murdered.

ANNIE. Oh dear.

PAIGE. I hope you're not going to ask me to recount every morbid detail of my mother's murder, are you? You wouldn't make me remember that, would you?

ANNIE. Oh no. Please. You don't have to.

PAIGE. Because it could make a person... depressed. And depressed people aren't good salesmen.

ANNIE. Here. *(Hands PAIGE the money.)* Honest, I'm sorry. I had no idea. I wouldn't have asked had I known.

(PAIGE goes to leave, turns.)

PAIGE. I was six and men came into our house. She was in the kitchen dipping blue candles. They said she'd cheated them somehow. She denied it. Cursed them out. They dipped her hands in the hot wax, dumped it on her. When they left I went to her crying—"Mama, Mama." There was bright red blood, rolling over the blue wax. *(Beat.)* Anyway you sort of look like her. *(Beat.)*

ANNIE. Paige, can you come for lunch next Tuesday?

PAIGE. I don't know.

ANNIE. I'd like to invest...in your business, help you with inventory. You have an eye for beautiful things.

PAIGE. You think so?

ANNIE. You have a gift. Come and we'll talk more about it.

PAIGE. Maybe. I'll have to see.

ANNIE. Next Tuesday then. We'll have China tea and finger sandwiches.

(PAIGE exits. ANNIE studies her purchase.)

END OF PLAY

MASHED POTATOES

By
Elaine Berman

Mashed Potatoes was featured in "Octoberfest," an evening of plays produced by Ensemble Studio Theatre, New York City, 1992, and was a finalist in the Actors Theatre of Louisville National Ten-Minute Play Contest, 1992.

CHARACTERS

BETH GREEN: A fairly well-dressed, polished woman in her 30s.

LEN ADAMS: A sophisticated man a few years older than Beth.

Beth and Len have been good friends for a long time.

SETTING: A large kitchen in a weekend house that was a farmhouse. There is no need for this to be a realistic set, but props should be real. The "stove" is downstage. When it is used, the actors face the audience. On the stove there are one large and one medium-sized pot. There is a side table and on it is a silver serving bowl with a lid.

TIME: The present.

MASHED POTATOES

AT THE CURTAIN: *BETH GREEN is putting the lid on the silver bowl. LEN ADAMS enters. It is his house, and he is very comfortable in the kitchen.*

BETH *(indicates the silver bowl).* There are the string beans. The mashed potatoes will be five more minutes.

LEN. What?

BETH. It's my fault.

LEN. What happened?

BETH. I timed it wrong. The string beans got done, but the potatoes didn't; I put them on too late. I've never made mashed potatoes for so many people. It took a long time for the water to start boiling. It's boiling now. Five minutes.

LEN. Everything else is out on the buffet getting cold.

BETH *(hands him the silver bowl).* Take the string beans. Let everyone start, and I'll bring out the potatoes when they're ready. Five minutes.

LEN *(puts the bowl down).* The potatoes go with other things in the meal. If people have finished that food by the time the potatoes arrive, it won't be the dinner I planned. I like to have everything out when guests are called to the table.

BETH. I feel ridiculous. You did this whole incredible dinner and you gave me two jobs—string beans and potatoes—and I fucked up. I'm not great at food. I'm just not. I would like to be, but I'm not.

LEN. You should have known. It's the same as making a big pot of spaghetti for a group—you have to start the water early.

BETH. I've never made a big pot of spaghetti for a group.

LEN. Most people have had that experience.

BETH. When cooking for a group is going on, I almost always make the salad. I like to cut and peel and chop. Salad's good because you can't time it wrong and screw up the whole dinner.

LEN. You should have volunteered to make the salad, then, instead of things that could hold up the meal.

BETH. I can see that you're really very ...

LEN. You should have.

BETH. Catherine volunteered to make the salad before I could. I make salad dressing with shallots chopped up into the teeniest little pieces, which creates a subtle, somewhat mysterious crunch. It's terrific, really.

LEN. If Catherine got the part you like, you didn't have to do anything.

BETH. I thought what can I do to string beans and mashed potatoes? How can I mess them up? I forgot about timing. I'm sorry, Len—all your beautiful food on the buffet getting cold because of my potatoes. If it weren't for me, this dinner would be perfectly timed. Everything you do is so accomplished. You are so accomplished, it makes me feel like a slob.

LEN. I don't mean, in any way, to make you feel like a slob. I'm very sorry about that. Do other people make you feel like a slob?

BETH. Only you.

LEN. Well, that's awful. Am I judgmental? Is that it?

BETH. No, you're not judgmental. If you were judgmental, you would be more flawed, and I wouldn't feel I was up against something so formidable.

LEN. Up against? You feel like you're up against something with me?

BETH. Not exactly up against. I used the wrong words.

LEN. What are the right words?

BETH. I don't know.

LEN. Could I improve by becoming less formidable?

BETH. You should stay as you are. I'm the one who has to improve. I mean if I volunteer to make mashed potatoes for Thanksgiving dinner, I should know when to start them. Ah, Len, you've got sweet potatoes out there. Take the string beans and let everyone start. Please. We'll dump the damn mashed potatoes. Who'll know the difference?

LEN. You might have asked me. I thought you were waiting a long time to start the water boiling.

BETH. Then why didn't you say something?

LEN. You complain when I tell you what to do.

BETH. You can tell me things like "Get the water boiling now for the potatoes." I have no pride about something like that. I don't have to prove anything with food; I just want to perform adequately.

LEN. That other pot. That's the milk warming, right?

BETH. What milk warming?

LEN. The milk for the potatoes.

BETH. It should be warm?

LEN. Of course.

BETH. I've never heard of that.

LEN. It's the secret of good mashed potatoes.

BETH. That's the pot from the string beans. My mother always used milk straight from the refrigerator.

LEN (*pokes into the big pot with a fork to test the potatoes for doneness*). Everyone's mother did that.

BETH. That's what I do. I put butter in first, while the hot potatoes will melt it. Then milk, then salt and pepper.

LEN. If the milk is hot, it doesn't make the potatoes cold. (*He tastes a little piece of potato from the pot.*) I'll drain these. Heat the milk.

BETH. If we use cold milk, we can get these potatoes out there in two minutes, before everything else is ice cold.

LEN. Beth, please, let's do it right. (*He begins to drain the potatoes.*)

BETH. No! Len, please! Let's do it wrong!

LEN. Heat the milk.

(*A beat, then BETH goes to the refrigerator.*)

LEN. These potatoes are a little overcooked. They didn't have to cook quite so long.

BETH (*at the refrigerator, pouring milk into a small pot*). We were both in here!

LEN. Just a tad. Nothing serious.

BETH. I also like to make coleslaw. It's really tough to ruin that. It's even harder to ruin than salad. With coleslaw you can't undercook or overcook anything. (*She puts the pot of milk on the stove.*)

LEN. I've had your coleslaw. You could shred it a little more finely.

BETH. What?

LEN. Of course, that's just a matter of preference. *(LEN is mashing potatoes, and he'll put in butter and salt and carefully grind pepper in.)*

BETH. You think so? You think my coleslaw should be shredded more finely?

LEN. I said it's a matter of taste.

BETH. You make coleslaw. Do you think yours is better than mine?

LEN. It's not better, Beth. I didn't say better. This isn't a contest. We're not having a coleslaw cook-off.

BETH *(almost shouting)*. All right!

LEN. Mine is simply shredded more finely, and I enjoy it more that way. I think most people do. The secret is in the knife. You need a very sharp knife.

BETH. Very sharp...

LEN. I have a number of first-rate knives. Remind me, I'll give you one.

BETH. All right. I'll use your knife to shred the cabbage more finely when I make coleslaw. Thanks, Len, I'm learning a lot from you today. Make mashed potatoes with warm milk, shred cabbage for coleslaw into little bitty skinny shreds with an extremely sharp knife. Thanks.

LEN. There's nothing wrong with your ability to cook. You just don't concentrate, because you're not interested.

BETH. I liked cooking when I had roommates. Working in the kitchen with other people is fun.

LEN. These are a little mealy.

BETH. Is that my fault?

LEN. No, and I can cover it up with some extra butter.

BETH. Good. Do that. Cover it up. But even with other people, I'm not great. One time I claimed potato salad as a specialty and made it for a party. I forgot to put salt in the water. It was remarkably tasteless—something like mayonnaise and celery on gym socks.

LEN (*comforting her*). You're oversensitive about things like this. I'll bet it wasn't really that bad.

BETH. It was.

LEN. You could solve the whole cooking situation by sticking to green salad with your special dressing.

BETH. You think I'm so hopeless? You think I can't learn?

LEN. Why learn if it doesn't interest you?

BETH. I always think someday I will become interested. I feel it's wonderful to have the ability to offer good food to people. I don't dislike cooking or anything like that. I like to read recipes. I just have my mind on other things right now.

LEN. So you can't cook. So what?

BETH. Don't make me sound hopeless, Len.

LEN. Maybe you should just stick to salad.

BETH. That might be true, but I don't like the way it sounds.

LEN. It is true.

BETH. And maybe you should stick those mashed potatoes up your ass.

LEN. I beg your pardon...

BETH. Bad idea?

LEN. Have I done something?

BETH. You make me feel bad, that's all. You make me feel small. Some people make me feel like more; you make me feel like less. It has something to do with how accomplished you are, but that's not exactly it. I know accomplished people who make me feel great.

LEN. How's that milk coming?

BETH. It's warm.

LEN. Dump it in here.

BETH *(dumping the milk into the pot of mashed potatoes)*. It's not that I don't like you.

LEN *(mashing potatoes)*. Yeah.

BETH. Love you even. It's not that I don't love you. You know? But you make me feel like crap a lot of the time.

LEN. I don't mean to. Hey, taste these potatoes! See what the warm milk does?

BETH *(tastes)*. Wonderful. They're wonderful potatoes.

LEN. They are sensational.

BETH. You did it again, Len. Better get them on the table. *(BETH picks up the silver bowl of string beans to carry to the buffet.)*

LEN *(turns his attention from the potatoes to BETH)*. I think we have to work on this. I mean really work on it. Do something about it. You are important to me. If I make you feel like crap a lot of the time, we should work on it.

BETH. I don't know if we can.

LEN. Now you're saying I'm hopeless, but I'm not. If you think I am, you don't know me very well. Where were you going to put the potatoes?

BETH. Where?

LEN. What vessel?

BETH. Vessel?

LEN. Dish, bowl, platter...

BETH. I don't know.

LEN. You didn't plan ahead?

BETH *(clutching the silver bowl)*. It's your house. I thought you'd come up with something. Oh, God, what is wrong with me? I can't even plan ahead for a potato vessel.

LEN. We'll talk later. *(Looks in cabinet.)* I have a silver bowl. We'll talk later. Don't worry about it. It's just fine. No problem. Where's that bowl? That silver bowl. Where is it? *(He looks up.)* You're standing there holding it! The string beans are in it! Why didn't you say so?

BETH *(looks down and is amazed when she realizes she is holding the bowl. She puts it down).* Oh, God, I am. I am holding it. Len, I'm going home.

LEN. You shouldn't miss this dinner.

BETH. I'm going right now. Don't call me.

LEN. Right, it'll be too late when...

BETH. Don't ever call me.

LEN. My plain white bowl will do. It will have to; I've used the rest...and I think you're being silly.

BETH. Don't say that! *(She reaches into the pot of mashed potatoes, takes a handful and puts it in LEN's face.)*

LEN. Beth!

BETH. Len, Happy Thanksgiving.

(BETH goes out.)

END OF PLAY

UNDRESS ME CLARENCE

By

Doug Grissom

Undress Me Clarence was staged by Offstage Theatre, Charlottesville, Va., in 1998, and by Offstage Boston in 1999.

CHARACTERS

HE: A man.
SHE: A woman.

Note: The characters should give no hint of sexual arousal.

SETTING: A bar.
TIME: The present.

UNDRESS ME CLARENCE

AT THE CURTAIN: *A man and a woman are sitting at a bar. The man is reading a newspaper.*

SHE. Undress me, Clarence.

HE. Excuse me?

SHE. Undress me with your eyes.

HE. Now?

SHE. Yes.

HE. Can I finish this?

SHE. Clarence!

HE. Okay, okay. *(HE puts down his paper, stares at her.)*

SHE. Well?

HE. Well what? I'm doing it.

SHE. I want a blow-by-blow.

HE. Okay. I'm down to your cream-colored brassiere.

SHE. That's not fair.

HE. What isn't?

SHE. You can't start in the middle like that. I don't want to miss anything. Start over.

HE. All right. Let's see. Should I start the way I started before, or should I take a new approach?

SHE. What was your old approach?

HE. I was beginning at the top and working down. See I could begin at the shoes and work up. Or I could be exotic and start at the underwear and work out.

SHE. Just make it the way it's best for you.

HE. Okay. Your blouse is coming off...

SHE. What do you mean "coming off"—what's it doing, vaporizing or something?

HE. I don't know, it's just removed.

SHE. That's absurd. You should be seeing exactly what's happening to every article of clothing.

HE. Well, should I be in it, then? Should I be watching myself undress you? Or should there be another force doing it? A cyborg, perhaps?

SHE. It's your fantasy; if cyborgs *arouse* you—

HE. No, no—I'll do it. Okay. All right. There I am. I'm unbuttoning the top button. Now the second, third and fourth. I pause a moment, spreading out what I've just unbuttoned. Now I can see your cream-colored brassiere—

SHE. That really bothers me.

HE. What?

SHE. It shouldn't be *cream-colored.*

HE. Well I can't tell what you're really wearing—

SHE. I'm not talking about what I'm really wearing, it's none of your business what I'm really wearing, I'm talking about fantasy—what kind of a man fantasizes about a cream-colored brassiere?

HE. What are you saying?

SHE. You know what I'm saying.

HE. Okay it's green.

SHE. Green?

HE. Black!

SHE. Fine. Black *lace*, maybe.

HE. Fine. Now I can see your black *lace* brassiere. I then continue and unbutton the fifth and sixth buttons. Again I spread what I've uncovered. Your stomach is moving rhythmically. I unbutton the seventh and last button, I open your shirt wide, drape it over your shoulders, and it slips to the floor. Your white arms form slight goose pimples.

SHE. Goose bumps.

HE. What?

SHE. Goose bumps. Make them goose bumps.

HE. Very well. Your white arms form slight goose bumps. Now I have to decide whether to continue by fully exposing your torso or start unraveling your lower extremities.

SHE. *Yes;* so decide.

HE. Okay, I've got it. I gently unhinge the belt that holds your skirt up, slide the end of the belt out through the buckle, and completely loosen the belt. I expect the skirt to fall. It doesn't. I notice the three...um... watchamacallits.

SHE. Snaps.

HE. Yes; um— Thank you. The three snaps and proceed to unsnap them. Snap. Snap. *(Slight pause)* Snap. I loosen the skirt. It wafts to the floor.

SHE. It does what?

HE. It wafts...it falls gracefully...to the floor.

SHE. Oh.

HE. Your legs are more beautiful than I imagined. Again slight goose pimples—goose *bumps*—seem to form. And now you are standing there in your non-cream-colored brassiere and red lace panties.

SHE. Black no lace.

HE. Black no-lace panties.

SHE. Do you have an erection?

HE. Me?

SHE. Yes you.

HE. The me talking to you or the me undressing you?

SHE. The me undressing you—I mean the *you* undressing *me*.

HE. Well of course.

SHE. When did it happen?

HE. While I was undressing you.

SHE. Is it so much to ask for a little specificity here?

HE. All right! A slight erection started when I undid the first four buttons—was it four or five?

SHE. I don't know.

HE. When I undid the first four or five buttons on your blouse, I developed a slight erection.

SHE. What exactly is a slight erection?

HE. Let's just say I felt movement. I felt even more movement when your blouse wafted to the floor. However, the movement stopped and receded when I realized you weren't wearing a cream-colored brassiere but instead were all tarted up in a black lace bra—

SHE. Hey!

HE. But don't worry, the movement only temporarily receded and there was once again movement when your skirt wafted—that means falls gently—to the floor and when I see your beautifully formed legs there is the beginning of rigidity and when I glance up and see your black no-lace panties I am a steel rod. All right, now we're caught up, right?

SHE. Right.

HE. Right. Another decision. Oh wait, I forgot. I bend down, take off your shoes. All right, now the decision.

SHE. Is that all about the shoes?

HE. Yes.

SHE. No goose bumps or anything?

HE. Yes fine; you have the only feet in the world that form goose bumps—all right?

SHE. I was only saying—

HE. Hush. Now what should be revealed first? The torso or the lower extremities.

SHE. Don't be so clinical.

HE. The boobs or the—

SHE. Don't be vulgar.

HE. Might as well be traditional. I put my hands on your shoulders and gently turn you around. Your brassiere has two hooks; I unhook the first, take a slight pause: the second. I put my hands in the center of your back and spread them. As my hands spread across your shoulders they float the straps down your arms. You straighten your arms very slightly—

SHE. No.

HE. What?

SHE. I don't straighten my arms. I don't do anything.

HE. Fine. I grab each strap and guide it down each arm until the *force of gravity* pulls it gently to the floor. I run the back of my right hand down the center of your back. You quiver slightly—*involuntarily*; with your back still to me I bend down and grasp the lace border of your panties and pull them gently—

SHE. You're using gently too much.

HE. I pull them gingerly to the floor.

SHE. I don't like that.

HE. I pull them—I pull them; why are panties plural—it's only one after all—

SHE. Don't digress please.

HE. I pull them eagerly to the floor.

SHE. I don't like that either but go on.

HE. I pull them eagerly to the floor. The white skin of your buttocks—

SHE. No.

HE. Derriere?

SHE. No.

HE. Ass?

SHE. Good God no.

HE. Well what then? —I'm out of ideas.

SHE. Oh, just say "back there."

HE. Very well. The white skin of your "back there" clashes exquisitely with the rest of your body.

SHE. I thought I was white all over.

HE. Well, yes, in comparison with—I mean—the extra-pale white skin of your "back there" clashes slightly but exquisitely with your white but ever-so-slightly darker rest of your body, all right!?

SHE. Fine.

HE. Okay. I stand up—

SHE. You've been sitting?

HE. I was kneeling down to grab your panties—

SHE. No; did you say that?

HE. *Yes.* I stand up from my *formerly kneeling* position. I turn you around. The effect is of course breathtaking, stunning and breathtaking. There you are: well-turned ankles, upturned breasts, legs turned—some way or other—creamy skin, beautiful "back there," pubic hair thick and rich—

SHE. That sounds like a milk shake—

HE. Pubic hair fluffy and downy—

SHE. That's a pillow!

HE. Pubic hair looking very...*pubic*! My heart and other organs are pounding! I'm a steel rod of desire—

SHE. You were a steel rod before.

HE. I'm even more of a steel rod—I'm an even steeler rod—I'm a steel rod the likes of which has never been seen in the world of steel—*I'm a metallurgical marvel of steelness—I—*

SHE. I got the point!

HE. So to speak!

SHE. You're ruining this!! Why are you ruining this? Is this so much to ask!? That you do this little thing for me? Is it so much to ask that you just be a little... that you be just be a little tiny bit...

HE. I'm sorry. Let me try once more. Can I try once more?

SHE. Who's stopping you?

HE. I stand up, put my hand on your shoulders and turn you around. And there you are. For the first time I really see you. Not just your body. The body I've seen many, many times before. But you. The essence of you beyond the body. And that's truly stunning. And that excites. No. That profoundly thrills me. I now know a passion beyond what I've ever imagined. I'm breathing hard, my heart is pounding. I reach out for you and...

(SHE has her head back, eyes closed, enjoying this. HE watches her and seems to really feel something for the first time. Pause. Then HE sits down, picks up his newspaper.)

SHE. ...and then what?

HE. Then nothing. I'm finished. You asked me to undress you with my eyes and I did. You're naked; that's it.

SHE. Oh. Yeah. 'Course. I just... almost thought that...

HE. Something might actually happen?

SHE. Yeah.

HE. That there might be some real connection?

SHE. Yeah.

HE. Now that's a *real* fantasy.

(They BOTH laugh. They stop laughing. They look at each other for a beat and then turn away.)

SHE. Clarence. I'm still naked. You left me naked. I'm cold. Clarence. I'm *cold.*

END OF PLAY

TRUTH AND SEX

By

Susan Cinoman

Truth and Sex premiered in an evening of short plays entitled "Cinoman and Rebeck" at the Miranda Theatre in New York City in 1994.

<u>CHARACTERS</u>

KEITH:
LAURIE: — Young lovers in their late 20s.

SETTING: A bare stage serving as a sidewalk in front of a movie theatre, and a table and two chairs to serve as a restaurant.

TIME: The present. Late at night.

TRUTH AND SEX

AT THE CURTAIN: *KEITH and LAURIE have just come out of a movie theatre late at night.*

KEITH. Do you want to get some coffee or something?

LAURIE. Or something.

KEITH. You're bad.

LAURIE. Oh? Well, you're good.

KEITH. Yes.

LAURIE. You're the best.

KEITH. That's what you keep telling me.

LAURIE. Do you believe it?

KEITH. I don't know. You'll have to keep it up.

LAURIE. Mmmm. I'll try.

KEITH. Let's get coffee first. Do you know someplace?

LAURIE. Yes. (*LAURIE touches KEITH suggestively as she leads him in the direction of a coffee bar.*) Do we have to?

KEITH. Evil.

LAURIE. Sordid.

KEITH. Twisted.

LAURIE. Sick.

KEITH. Perverse.

LAURIE. I can't help it. I get very turned on when I see *Miracle on 34th Street.* Here?

(*LAURIE has led KEITH to the restaurant through their walking and kissing.*)

KEITH. Perfect.

LAURIE. It's toasty.

KEITH. This is the perfect place. Great choice.

LAURIE. Thanks.

KEITH. I didn't even know this place existed. How do you find these places?

LAURIE. I don't know.

KEITH. You always seem to do it though. Especially for Chinese.

LAURIE. Well...

KEITH. So why do you get turned on watching *Miracle on 34th Street*?

LAURIE. Oh I don't know. Christmas, I guess. The lights and all. I get excited.

KEITH. Huh.

LAURIE. You think that's strange?

KEITH. Well...I mean it's a classic. The movie. But you know...the whole thing is kind of schmaltzy. I mean... yeah it's a bit strange. I can't find the erotic appeal.

LAURIE. Schmaltzy?

KEITH. Schmaltzy. It's Jewish. It means like...big emotions. Overdone.

LAURIE. Oh. Uh-huh. Uh-huh. So do you want to go home and have sex?

KEITH. I'd sort of like to just enjoy this coffee for a while.

LAURIE. Don't you have coffee at home?

KEITH. Yes.

LAURIE. So?

KEITH. I don't really feel like going home yet.

LAURIE. Oh.

KEITH. Laurie...

LAURIE. Is it because I'm not a blonde?

KEITH. What?

LAURIE. If I were a blonde would you want to take me home with you right away?

KEITH. You mean you're not a blonde? And all this time I thought you were a young Shelley Winters.

LAURIE. Shelley Winters? Why do you mention Shelley Winters?

KEITH. I was kidding.

LAURIE. But why Shelley Winters?

KEITH. She was a blonde.

LAURIE. So was Marilyn Monroe. And Veronica Lake. Why did you think of Shelley Winters?

KEITH. I don't know.

LAURIE. Because she was Jewish?

KEITH. I don't know. Because she was Jewish?

LAURIE. Just tell me.

KEITH. Because I saw *The Poseidon Adventure* on TV last night.

LAURIE. Oh.

KEITH. Because she was Jewish?

LAURIE. Just wondering.

KEITH. Shelley Winters was Jewish?

LAURIE. Is Jewish.

KEITH. I didn't know she was.

LAURIE. Is. She's not dead, just Jewish.

KEITH. Laurie, the reason I want to stay is because we have sex a lot.

LAURIE. I know.

KEITH. A real lot.

LAURIE. So?

KEITH. So for the past three months it's been nothing but steady, unrelenting sex.

LAURIE. And you're unhappy with it.

KEITH. No. I'm very happy. I'm ecstatic. It's like I died and went to sex heaven.

LAURIE. But now you've tired of me and you want out.

KEITH. Out of sex heaven? I don't think so.

LAURIE. Then what?

KEITH. I want to talk to you. I want to know you better.

LAURIE. I told you everything already.

KEITH. Everything.

LAURIE. Yes.

KEITH. Then why do I feel like you're keeping something from me?

LAURIE. It's your Catholic guilt. You can't let yourself be happy.

KEITH. What about your Catholic guilt?

LAURIE. What about it?

KEITH. What is your guilt not letting you confess?

LAURIE. Nothing.

KEITH. Something.

LAURIE. No.

KEITH. You're tearing up a linen napkin.

LAURIE. There's nothing more to tell.

KEITH. You never told me anything about your parents.

LAURIE. I don't think about my parents when I'm in bed with you. Do you think about your parents?

KEITH. Yes.

LAURIE. You do?

KEITH. I sometimes think about them. Not when we're in bed. But I sometimes think about them. And I sometimes mention them. And you have never mentioned them ... yours.

LAURIE. Oh.

KEITH. Why not? Are they in the mob? Are they vampires?

LAURIE. They are just regular old parents. And that's it. There's nothing more.

KEITH. Nothing.

LAURIE. No.

KEITH. Well...I'd like to meet them sometime.

LAURIE. Fine.

KEITH. OK.

LAURIE. Fine. Fine.

KEITH. OK then. We will.

LAURIE. I'm Jewish.

KEITH. Very funny.

LAURIE. I am.

KEITH. Come on.

LAURIE. I know what schmaltz means, Keith. And kvetch. And a lot of other words, too. And that's how I know where all the good Chinese restaurants are, OK? Are you satisfied?

KEITH. But you told me you were Irish and a little bit Delaware Indian.

LAURIE. I've been saying that since high school.

KEITH. Delaware Indian?

LAURIE. I like Delaware Indian. They built a transportation system all over the East Coast before they were pushed out by the Europeans.

KEITH. You're Jewish?

LAURIE. Yes.

KEITH. You lied to me.

LAURIE. Sort of.

KEITH. Did you go to Little Flower?

LAURIE. No.

KEITH. But you said you went to Little Flower.

LAURIE. My best friends all went there. It sounded like fun.

KEITH. You thought Catholic school sounded like fun?

LAURIE. Yes.

KEITH. Then you must be Jewish.

LAURIE. And my best friends were all blondes.

KEITH. So?

LAURIE. So. You know how men are with blondes. Men worship blondes.

KEITH. Oh God.

LAURIE. I thought that you would prefer them.

KEITH. Who?

LAURIE. My Catholic girlfriends.

KEITH. You'll have to introduce me first.

LAURIE. Thanks a lot.

KEITH. I'm angry.

LAURIE. Me too. Do you want to go to bed now?

KEITH. No. I want to know why you lied to me.

LAURIE. I told you.

KEITH. What else did you lie about?

LAURIE. You hate me.

KEITH. No. I don't.

LAURIE. You do. You're anti-Semitic.

KEITH. What?

LAURIE. I guess this is over.

KEITH. Is that what you want?

LAURIE. What do you think?

KEITH. I think you're still lying to me.

LAURIE. I changed my whole identity for you.

KEITH. You said you've been lying about this since high school.

LAURIE. Right.

KEITH. So. You didn't change your identity. Your identity is to lie about your religion.

LAURIE. But I just told you the truth, so I have changed my identity.

KEITH. Oh.

LAURIE. Stupid.

KEITH. Are you hiding anything else?

LAURIE. Like what?

KEITH. I don't know. You can't hide out in bed anymore, Laurie. You have to tell the truth.

LAURIE. But you haven't told me the truth.

KEITH. Me? I'm not Jewish.

LAURIE. Not that truth. The truth of how you feel.

KEITH. The truth of how I feel?

LAURIE. Yes.

KEITH. About you.

LAURIE. Please.

KEITH. How I do feel about a woman who I've been seeing who I thought was a nice Irish Catholic girl with an insatiable sexual appetite and I discover she's been lying about a major aspect of her life because her insecurity has compelled her to come up with the twisted fiction that she'd have been better off as a blonde, Catholic American Indian?

LAURIE. Yes.

KEITH. I'm in love with you.

LAURIE. Oh. (*Pause.*) Good.

KEITH. So. Do you want to go home and have sex now?

LAURIE. Actually, I kind of feel like a slice of pie and coffee.

END OF PLAY

TAKING OFF

By
Adam Kraar

Taking Off was written for Primary Stages' "America Project" and was given a reading there in 1996. The play was premiered by Heartland Stage in Muncie, Ind., in 1998.

CHARACTERS

MIRIAM: 42.
MARTY: 16, son of Miriam and Herbert.
HERBERT: 43.
FERN: 12, Marty's sister.

SETTING: The airport in the Republic of Singapore.
TIME: 1972.

TAKING OFF

AT THE CURTAIN: *MIRIAM, MARTY, HERBERT and FERN stand in a waiting area at the Singapore Airport.*

VOICE ON LOUDSPEAKER. Singapore Airlines Flight 95 is now boarding at Gate A6.

MIRIAM. If it gets really cold, wear the blue parka—and put the hood up.

HERBERT. Here's the traveler's checks. Sign each one here now, and then when you use it, sign here.

MIRIAM. You've got to watch out for frostbite. You wanna lose an ear? Don't wear the hood.

MARTY. I'll wear it.

MIRIAM. Why are you cracking your knuckles? Are you nervous?

MARTY *(nervously; with false lightness)*. No!

HERBERT. I've deposited three hundred dollars in your school account. You can draw on that for anything you need, but charge your books. If you need more, get in touch.

MARTY. Um, I'm sure that's more than—

HERBERT. It's not for goodies. You may need clothes—

MIRIAM. Herbert, he's got clothes—he's got two trunks full of clothes—

FERN. Look at the board. Flight 7—Delayed.

HERBERT. No announcement, no explanation—I could expect this in Delhi or even Bangkok—

MIRIAM. Mai Pen Rai.

FERN *(she's heard it over the years)*. What does that mean?

MIRIAM. "Never mind." *(To MARTY.)* So, how do you feel, Mr. Going Off to America?

MARTY. Good. Great! Uh...I'll miss you guys, of course. —Oh God.

MIRIAM. What?

MARTY *(searching through all his pockets)*. My ear- drops!

HERBERT. For crying out loud!

(MARTY tilts his head and pounds the top of it.)

MIRIAM. His ears are already filling up! *(She clamps her fingers on MARTY's nose.)* Here: blow. Just blow!

MARTY *(blows. Then)*. Ah. All clear. Thanks.

MIRIAM. What is he gonna do without eardrops?

HERBERT. There's nothing we can do now. He'll have to get some in New York.

MARTY. I'm fine!

MIRIAM. Oh, Son. I know you hate this, but I'm gonna miss you!

MARTY. I'll be back!

MIRIAM. You'll never really be back.

HERBERT. Miriam, what on earth do you mean by that?

MIRIAM. My baby is leaving home!

MARTY. *Mom.*

MIRIAM. Sorry. Sorry.

HERBERT. If there's ever an emergency and you can't reach us, call your grandparents.

MIRIAM. Oh, Herbert, are we doing the right thing?

MARTY. I'm going to be perfectly fine. I'll wear the hood and come back with both ears intact.

MIRIAM. Marty, if they ask you to register for the draft—

HERBERT. Miriam, he's sixteen years old.

MIRIAM. So, time goes quickly, this war goes quickly— If they ask you to register for the draft tell them you've become a Quaker.

HERBERT. Miriam, that's perjury.

MIRIAM. Well maybe he'll become a Quaker. God knows we never gave him any religious training.

FERN. Yeah, how come we're not Christians if we have Christmas? Is Grandaddy mad 'cause we're not Jewish?

HERBERT. No.

MIRIAM. He's not happy about it. But Daddy doesn't care what his father thinks of him. —You won't sign up for the draft, will you? You could be killed. And you would have to kill.

MARTY. I...don't think it will come to that.

HERBERT. He's right. Nixon's got to pull those troops out.

MIRIAM. You go to Canada. If they ever want to draft you. Promise me. *(Beat.)* Promise—or I won't let you leave.

MARTY. If I'm drafted, I'll file for non-combat status. I'll get an assignment as a headliner for Bob Hope. Okay?

HERBERT. This is a very good school. Seventy percent of the faculty have advanced degrees. Ninety percent of the students go on to college.

MIRIAM. And it was one of the first co-ed boarding schools in the country.

FERN. Is Marty gonna get a girlfriend?

MIRIAM. He might. Marty: do you have any last-minute questions about...sex?

MARTY. No!

HERBERT. You know they advance the clocks over there—Daylight Savings Time—

MIRIAM. For God's sake, Herbert, he knows.

HERBERT. Do you?

MARTY. Eastern, Central, yes.

FERN. Will you get the Herman's Hermits poster? The one I showed you in the magazine?

HERBERT. He's not going to have time to look for posters.

MIRIAM. He can't work all the time. What he needs to focus on are his human skills.

FERN. You know what I think? I think Marty is going to marry a black woman. Because he's always reading about the civil rights, and he wants to go into politics.

MIRIAM. He could be President. But I think you're reconsidering your presidential ambitions, aren't you?

MARTY. I plan to be a renaissance man. Do many things. I may yet run.

MIRIAM. Leonardo, Fellini and JFK rolled into one— My God, Herbert, we shoulda raised him Catholic.

FERN. Can Catholics marry blacks?

MIRIAM. Fern, some Catholics are blacks; and some blacks are Catholics.

FERN. Don't ya think, Marty, you might?

MARTY. Might what?

FERN. Marry a black woman.

MARTY (*snapping, showing a bit of his exasperation*). I don't know!

MIRIAM. If you go to the city, be careful. Don't go into dark alleys.

HERBERT. He knows.

MARTY *(to FERN)*. I could probably get that poster for you in town.

FERN. Thanks!

VOICE ON LOUDSPEAKER. Singapore Airlines Flight 7 to New York is now boarding at Gate 2A.

MARTY. I got a few little gifts for everybody.

MIRIAM. You didn't have to do that!

MARTY. Mom, here's a collection of my political essays—

MIRIAM. Oh, Marty! And you autographed it! Thank you! Come here, you. I hope you find someone over there to hug you like this.

MARTY. You're welcome. *(Moving out of the hug.)* Dad: *(Gives him gift.)*

HERBERT. Look at this. It's a bottle opener, a corkscrew and a magnifying glass. Very nice. Thank you. *(HERBERT shakes MARTY's hand.)*

MARTY. Here, Fern. *(Gives her gift.)*

MIRIAM. What is it? Fern, what's the matter?

(FERN cries.)

MARTY. It's sugar cubes, for that horse you ride. What did I...?

FERN *(through tears)*. Thank you.

MARTY. What? Tell me, please.

FERN. I won't be riding Roxy anymore because...it's, it's okay, really.

MARTY. Because what?

MIRIAM. Well, your father's commissions the last two quarters—

HERBERT. Just tightening the belt a bit. A lot of little guys suddenly thought they could undersell us; they won't last. Once I get those sales up, she'll be back with Roxy. Speaking of which, I've got that meeting at six, so—

MIRIAM. Not yet.

FERN. Don't worry, Marty. I love these. *(FERN eats a sugar cube.)* Mm!

MARTY *(trying to return some of the traveler's checks)*. I really don't need all these traveler's—

MIRIAM. Marty: just take it. You never know. What if your plane is hijacked? —He might need ransom!

(HERBERT gives MIRIAM a stern look.)

FERN. What if you're unhappy when you get to Westfall? Will you leave? What if you don't like the people there? Your roommate? You've never shared a room before, have you? Are you scared?

MIRIAM. You don't have to do this. I mean, you can always change your mind.

HERBERT. He can't just change his mind.

MIRIAM. If it absolutely doesn't work out.

HERBERT. It'll work out. For two thousand dollars a year, it better work out.

MARTY *(nervously)*. Uh—I'm looking forward to this! Really! *(MARTY tilts his head and pounds the top of it a couple times.)*

MIRIAM. Marty: blow.

(MARTY holds his nose with his fingers and blows.)

MIRIAM. Please don't keep to yourself all the time. It's going to be a huge adjustment—

HERBERT. This school is going to fit him like a tailored suit.

MIRIAM. He hadn't heard of Herman's Hermits. He hasn't had school buddies he kept for years. Because he couldn't. Because we moved.

HERBERT. I think you're underestimating him.

MIRIAM. Herbert, don't take that tone with me.

HERBERT. Miriam.

FERN *(babyish)*. Don't be mad.

MIRIAM. I'm sorry, kids. I guess I didn't realize how hard... *(Starting to cry.)* this-was-all-going-to-be.

MARTY. I—I'll write. I'll be back in eight months. It's really not such a... long time.

MIRIAM. Remember the day we first left the States? You were seven. You got the last flight pin, and Fern was wailing. So you gave it to Fern. You remember?

MARTY *(changing the subject)*. They never hand out those pins anymore. The airlines just don't give you the same—

MIRIAM. They put this candied version of a redneck love song over the plane's loudspeakers—the planes were a lot noisier in 1961—and after we took off, the plane circled the skyscrapers and we passed the Statue of Liberty. It grabbed you, in the red dusk. A different dusk than a Jaipur dusk or a Singapore eight-thirty-three p.m. A New York, America dusk. America: land of protest, and commerce, and assassination. —Remember when Pete Seeger came to New Delhi?

(FERN sings "We Shall Overcome"; MIRIAM joins in.)

HERBERT. Okay, okay—you're making a scene.

MARTY. The sequel to *The Ugly American*—the Off-Key American.

(HERBERT and MARTY laugh.)

MIRIAM. We weren't off-key. Anyway, we were sitting in that TWA propeller plane, and while the speakers tinkled "Stand by Your Man," we banked toward the Statue and the sun filled her loving eyes. And tears started rolling down your cheeks. A rare public occurrence for a boy of seven. The stewardess was the first to notice. "Is there anything I can do?" You wouldn't say what was the matter. So I told her: "He's leaving home for a long time, and he's going to miss his friends—and he's going to miss America." ... You knew! You knew.

MARTY. ... What?

MIRIAM. You knew you'd never be the same again. Right?

(Pause.)

HERBERT. He's got to board his plane—

MIRIAM. Herbert! Just button it up!

HERBERT. I won't have you talking to me like that—

MIRIAM. We are not water-resistant Samsonite suitcases that you can just throw anywhere you please! You've hauled us all over Asia for ten years, and now your son is leaving home and all you can think about is your goddamn rush-hour traffic!

FERN. Mom! Dad!

HERBERT. People are staring. This is Singapore.

FERN. I'm sorry, Marty.

MARTY. It's okay. It's a ... big—step. For all of us.

MIRIAM. Yes!

VOICE ON LOUDSPEAKER. Ladies and gentlemen, singing is not permitted in the waiting area. —Singapore Airlines Flight 7 to Bahrain, London and New York boarding at Gate ... 2A. This is the final call.

MIRIAM. This is it. Oh, Marty.

HERBERT. Keep in touch.

MIRIAM. Call us—

HERBERT. The Bockstein's can telex us—

MIRIAM. The hell they will. He'll call, damn it, as soon as he lands.

MARTY. I'll call.

MIRIAM. You promise?

MARTY. Yes.

MIRIAM. I'm sorry. It's going to be fine. We're gonna be fine. It's all going to work out.

HERBERT. Of course it is.

MARTY. Thank you for this— [Opportunity]

HERBERT. You're quite welcome.

FERN. Goodbye, Marty. You don't have to hug me.

(MARTY quickly and awkwardly hugs her.)

MARTY. Hope you don't hit too much traffic on the way home.

HERBERT. Well, it's after five, so—but don't worry about it. You got your ticket? Have a great time.

MARTY. Watch out for those crazy cab drivers. Take care, Mom.

MIRIAM. Goodbye, Marty. Remember we love you.

MARTY. I will. I—I better board. Thank you. Well... Onward and upward! And I'll be back. ... 'Bye! *(He exits.)*

MIRIAM. He's off—to a strange new world.

END OF PLAY

ABOUT THE PLAYWRIGHTS

ERIC BERLIN was a member of the inaugural class of writers in the Julliard Playwriting Program. His plays include **The Star Attraction** and **The Perfect Thing**, both of which were developed in the Circle Rep Lab. **The Line That's Picked Up 1,000 Babes** and **The Midnight Moonlight Wedding Chapel**, published together as **Babes and Brides** (Samuel French), have been produced throughout the world.

ELAINE BERMAN has written film and video scripts, articles, educational materials and corporate training seminars. Her play, **Peacetime**, has been produced by the WPA Theatre, Capital Rep and the Playwright's Theatre of East Hampton. Her play for children, **Go Jump in the Lake** (Samuel French), was produced by the Long Wharf Theatre. Her other stage plays have been staged by Ensemble Studio Theatre, The Women's Wing, All Seasons Theatre Group, and others.

BARRY BRODSKY is the author of 25 plays that have been produced throughout the country, including Boston, New York and Los Angeles. He was a 2000 finalist in the Eugene O'Neill Theatre Center's National Playwrights Conference, and a two-time semi-finalist in the Chesterfield Film Writers Competition. He received an MFA in Playwriting from Brandeis University and teaches screenwriting at Emerson College and at the University of Massachusetts at Boston. He continues to be active in Playwrights Platform, a Boston-based playwriting group.

SUSAN CINOMAN has had her plays produced in New York City by Naked Angels, Creative Voices Theatre, the Miranda Theatre Company and Ensemble Studio Theatre. Her play, **Fitting Rooms**, was featured in *The Best Ameri-*

can *Short Plays of 1995-1996* (Applause Theatre Books). Her works have been directed by Jane Hoffman, Rob Decina, Jan Silverman, Valentina Fratti, and Suzann Brinkley, among others. She is a mother of two, a director and a teacher who lives in Connecticut.

LINDA EISENSTEIN has written numerous works for theatre and opera that have been produced regionally throughout the United States and internationally in Canada, England, Australia and South Africa. Her works include **Three the Hard Way** (Dramatic Publishing); **A Rustle of Wings**; the rock opera, **Star Wares: The Next Generation** and the musical, **The Last Red Wagon Tent Show in the Land**. **Rehearsing Cyrano** was recently produced by the National School of the Arts in Johannesburg, South Africa. She has also been featured in *The Best Stage Scenes of 1997*, published by Smith and Kraus, and *Even More Monologues for Women by Women*, published by Heinemann Books in 2001. She is a member of The Playwrights Unit at the Cleveland Play House.

HOPE GATTO previously worked in journalism and stand-up comedy before writing for the stage. After graduating from Mercer County Community College, she attended Kutztown University where she won the Bennett E. Harris Humorous Writing Award in 1995. Her plays have been produced in New York, New Jersey and Pennsylvania. She has worked for several years as a dramaturg for the playwriting program at the Passage Theater in Trenton, N.J. She resides in Hamilton, N.J., with her husband and their two children.

DOUG GRISSON is the head of playwriting at the University of Virginia. His plays have been produced by Theatre Virginia, the Source Theatre in Washington D.C., Mill Mountain Theatre in Roanoke, Va., Houston's Main

Street Theatre and the Venture Theatre in Philadelphia. He has won several awards, including the Virginia Playwriting Award (**Tocoi Light**), Mill Mountain New Play Competition (**Ned & Dan's History Emporium**) and the Outstanding New Play Award at the Washington Theatre Festival (**Year of Pilgrimage**). A piece dealing with teen sexual assault entitled **I Never Saw It Coming**, commissioned by the Sexual Assault Resource Agency and the Virginia Health Department, is touring high schools in Virginia and has played to over 6000 students. He is co-founder of Offstage Theatre, an organization committed to producing site-specific new work in non-theatrical spaces.

NANCY HANNA was a 2000 finalist for the Eugene O'Neill Theatre Center's National Playwrights Conference. Her play, **Away the Bear**, won the 1998 Regent University playwriting competition and has been produced in Virginia and Vancouver. **The Psalm of Edie Catz** has received readings at the Deep Ellum Center for the Arts in Dallas, Texas, and at Circle Theatre in Chicago. It was workshopped at the Lambs Player's Theatre in San Diego, Calif. Her work appears in *Scenes and Monologues for Young Actors* published by Dramatic Publishing. She lives in Chicago with her husband and three children.

NIKKI HARMON is a native New Yorker and the author of 25 plays running the gamut from political satires to murderous comedies. Her work has been produced throughout the United States, Canada, England and Australia. She has been a finalist for the Susan Smith Blackburn Prize and has won the Lee Korf Award, the Robert J. Pickering Award (twice), the Dayton Playhouse Competition, the Lawrence S. Epstein Award, Jacksonville University's Playwriting Award, and the Little Theatre of Alexandria National Award. An alumna of Carnegie Insitute of

Technology (Carnegie Mellon), she is also a stage manager, lighting designer and an award-winning artist.

OLGA HUMPHREY is an award-winning playwright whose recent play, **F-Stop,** was produced by New Directions Theater in New York City. Her works have also been produced by Ensemble Studio Theatre and Love Creek Productions in New York City, Moving Arts Theater in Los Angeles, Red Rocks Theater in Lakewood, Colo., and Pandora's Box in Buffalo, New York. She was co-winner of the Perishable Theatre's 1998 Women's Playwriting Festival for **Svetlana's New Flame** and won that theater's 1999 contest for **Hyperactive.** Her play, **Flambé,** was chosen for the Dionysia Festival held in The Netherlands in 1999. Her published works include **The Exception** and **Fire Works! Three Short Comedies** (Dramatic Publishing) and scenes and monologues in *Best Stage Scenes of 1997* and *Best Women's Monologues of 1997* (Smith and Kraus).

JULIE JENSEN is a recent recipient of a McKnight Fellowship at The Playwrights Center in Minneapolis and an NEA/TCG Residency Grant at Salt Lake Acting Company in Salt Lake City, Utah. **Last Lists of My Mad Mother,** winner of the Mill Mountain Theatre New Play Competition, has been produced frequently throughout the country and published by Dramatic Publishing. **Two-Headed,** commissioned by A.S.K. Theatre Projects, has been produced in New York and Los Angeles. **The Lost Vegas Series,** winner of the Jefferson Award, was produced in Chicago and London.

ADAM KRAAR was the 1998-1999 Playwriting Fellow at Manhattan Theatre Club, and has won playwriting awards and fellowships from Southeastern Theatre Conference, Aspen Playwrights Competition, Montana Repertory's

Missoula Colony, the Millay Colony and the Sewanee Writers Conference. His works have been produced in New York at Ensemble Studio Theatre, HB Playwrights Foundation, Alice's Fourth Floor, Abington Theatre, Theatreworks U.S.A., Todo Con Nada and the Phil Bosakowski Theatre. He has been produced regionally at the Illinois Theatre Center, N.Y. State Theatre Institute, and Raleigh Ensemble, among others. He grew up in India, Thailand, Singapore and the United States, earned an MFA from Columbia University, and lives in Brooklyn with his wife, Karen.

SETH KRAMER is a New York-based playwright whose work has been widely produced throughout the country. He has won numerous awards including the George R. Kernodle Playwriting Award, the Kennedy Center's Meritorious Achievement Award for Playwrighting, the New York Thespian Award and a grant from the Peter S. Reed Foundation. For three years running, his work has been a finalist in the Actors Theatre of Louisville National Ten-Minute Play Contest. Several of his plays have been selected as either a winner or finalist by the Nantucket Play Festival, the City Theatre of Miami Competition and the Annual OffBeat New York Festival. **After the Beep**, a collection of short plays, is published by Dramatic Publishing.

CARTER LEWIS was literary manager and playwright-in-residence at Geva Theatre in New York and co-founder and resident playwright for Upstart Stage in Berkeley, Calif. His works have been produced by Syracuse Stage, Arizona Theatre Company, the Barter Theatre, Virginia Stage, the Berkshire Theatre Festival, Florida Stage, Studio Arena Theatre and the Royal Court Theatre in London, among others. He has won the Julie Harris-Beverly Hills Theatre Guild Playwriting Award, the Lois and Richard

Rosenthal New Play Prize, the L. Arnold Weissberger New Dramatists Playwriting Award, and has been a two-time nominee for the American Theatre Critics Award. His published work includes **Soft Click of a Switch** (Samuel French), **An Asian Jockey In Our Midst** (Meriwether Publishing Ltd.) and **The One-Eyed Man Is King** (Smith and Kraus).

QUINCY LONG is a member of Ensemble Studio Theatre, the New Dramatists and the HB Playwrights Unit. His most recent work includes **The Lively Lad, The Year of the Baby** and **The Joy of Going Somewhere Definite**. He has received commissions from the Mark Taper Forum, South Coast Repertory Theatre, Soho Repertory Theatre, A.S.K. Projects and the Sundance Children's Theatre. He has been produced by the Magic Theatre, the Atlantic Theater Company, EnGarde Arts, and Berkely Repertory Theatre, among others. In 1986 he won the ASCAP/Cole Porter prize for playwriting at the Yale School of Drama, was a runner up for the Kesselring Prize in 1993, and a finalist for the Outer Circle Drama Critics Award in 1994. In 1996 he won the Fund for New American Plays Award.

PATRICIA MONTLEY has written dramas, feminist satires, adaptations of Greek classics, epic theatre, musicals, and story theatre versions of Japanese and Native American folktales. Her works include **Finding the Flame, Juice, The Unveiling** and **Rachel Carson Between the Devil and the Deep Blue Sea**. She has received grants from the Pennsylvania Council on the Arts, the Shubert Foundation, the Mary Roberts Rinehart Foundation, and Warner Brothers. Her works have been published by Samuel French, Meriwether Publishing, Ltd., Heinemann Books, Applause Theatre Books and *Dramatics* magazine.

SANDRA PERLMAN is a member of The Cleveland Play House Playwrights Unit and has had 14 plays produced in the United States and Australia. Recent works include **In Search of Red River Dog**, which premiered at New Jersey Rep in 2000 and **Jocasta** which premiered at The Cleveland Play House in 2001. Her plays have been finalists at the Eugene O'Neill Theater Center's National Playwrights Conference and the Actors Theatre of Louisville National Ten-Minute Play Contest. The recipient of two Ohio Arts Council fellowships, she was the operations director for the first International Women Playwrights Conference in Buffalo, N.Y., in 1988.

RICHARD STRAND is the author of **The Bug** and **The Death of Zukasky**, both of which premiered at Actors Theatre of Louisville's Humana Festival. **Ten Percent of Molly Snyder** premiered at Steppenwolf Theatre, and **My Simple City** premiered at Chicago's Rivendell Ensemble and was nominated for best new script by both the American Drama Critics Association and the Joseph Jefferson Committee. Other productions include **Clown**, produced by Victory Gardens Theater and **The Lincoln Park Zoo** which premiered at Geva Theatre under the direction of Anthony Zerbe. **The Second-Story Man**, was developed at the Eugene O'Neill Theatre Center's National Playwrights Conference and premiered at the Cricket Theatre in Minneapolis. His works have been published by Samuel French, Dramatists Play Service, Heinemann Books and Applause Theatre Books. He lives in California with his wife, Mary Lynn, and teaches at Mt. San Antonio College.